D0839550

The Prayer Experiment

The Prayer Experiment

Prayer Principles from
THE SERMON ON THE MOUNT

Margaret Therkelsen

Wipf & Stock
PUBLISHERS
Eugene, Oregon

THE PRAYER EXPERIMENT
Prayer Principles from The Sermon on the Mount

ISBN 13: 978-1-55635-139-6

Manufactured in the U.S.A.

Dedication

To my beloved husband John, whose help was invaluable in preparing this manuscript.

To Koby Miller for reading the manuscript and to the many dear friends who have been a part of this praying community for over 25 years, I extend my heartfelt gratitude for all your love and prayers.

Contents

Preface

THE BASIS for this book is a series of teachings I did for our prayer community in the early 1990s on the theme of the prayer principles as found in the Sermon on the Mount. At that time the lessons were compiled in a workbook format at the request of those who had been present at the teachings. Because of the green cover the booklet had a nickname "The Little Green Book."

The present edition is an expanded version of those early lessons. For those who have read the workbook version I trust that this will be a helpful review. While for those for whom this will be a first reading may you find it challenging and helpful for your prayer life.

Introduction

FOR OVER twenty-five years it has been my great privilege to be a part of a weekly praying community. This group is an interdenominational and interracial gathering of people from all over the city and neighboring communities. In the course of teaching on the many aspects of prayer over the years this study has been unusually fruitful.

I learned from my mother the power of the "Laboratory Prayer Experiment." She had read of Alexis Carroll, a scientist living and working in the early 1900's. He said, "The greatest frontier left to man is in the reality of prayer." This is a monumental statement coming from a scientist in that day. So she began to take prayer into the laboratory of her daily life and experiment by applying the laws of Jesus in strict obedience in her day to day experiences. She found the "cause and effect" principle to be overwhelmingly evident when prayerfully applied. I saw her "enter" the laboratory of prayer in her daily experiences and as a lay scientist, delving into careful applications and procedures, she believed God, obeyed the principles, and trusted Him for the result. The answers were life changing for the people involved. She studied with great earnestness the urging of Jesus to obey the Love Commandments and many of the Biblical promises as the foundation of answered prayer. Reflecting on how I saw my mother take the Scripture into the laboratory of her daily life caused me to feel that this would be a wonderful experience for our group.

The experiment was a willingness to become more obedient, in and through the Holy Spirit, to a new dimension of surrender to the law of Divine love and other conditions of the promises as found in the Sermon on the Mount. The bedrock for all answered prayer *is* obedience to the spiritual principles that Jesus sets forth in His most influential message to the disciples and multitudes—*The Sermon on the Mount*, Matthew chapters 5 through 7.

This has been a daring and revealing journey that has been exciting and highly dangerous because individually, as well as corporately, we have stood naked in His pure and holy Presence. Seeing anew (and afresh) our condition, we have discovered our need in a new way. It is only the Holy Spirit in us who can live these Realities, but He indeed is Victor and able to bring us, in Jesus, to a new and larger place of love and peace. It is our hope and prayer that everyone who reads this will enter God's laboratory of prayer and find the amazing results of prayer and faith.

AUTHORS NOTE:

I realize that the order of the chapters for the Sermon on the Mount is developed in this study in reverse order; however there is a profound reason for this curious sequence. It was some time after we had begun meeting that we realized that judgment and criticism are deadly to answers to prayer, and deadly to realizing His presence. We all knew that we needed a deeper cleansing in this area. So the Holy Spirit led us to start with chapter 7 which is central to this theme, followed by Matthew 6 and 5. The strong message of the individual chapters remains crystal clear regardless of the order. God deeply honored this prayer experiment of seeking to stay filled with the love of God so there is no need for being critical.

Jesus' Love Rules over Criticism

*A new commandment I give unto you, that
you love one another as I have loved you.*[1]
John 13:34

BEING PART of a large prayer group is not easy. As we
have gone through the years new people and long time
members, have found the expansion to be a sign of God's
life and growth within this body of Christ. This shows we
are not a clique, praise God. We are not ingrown and self-
focused, though we have a long way to go in being totally
selfless. We have learned many lessons in allowing Jesus to
love through us. Jesus is yearning to manifest Himself more
and more in our lives and times of prayer.

God is seeking to do a work far beyond any of us.
Studies show that seven years is the normal length for a
prayer group because of the deepening demands of love
which Satan thwarts through personality conflicts and dis-
sension. Jesus alone can keep a group meeting weekly over
the years. God is calling us to a new place of love and obedience to His laws of love. This is a place of stretching and
growing that He might manifest His power in a new way in
and through us in prayer.

1. All Scripture references in this book are from the King James
Version of the Bible.

We have seen great and awesome answers over the years. It is thrilling and amazing to be a part of God's life through the life of prayer! He has worked in spite of us to bless others and ourselves. But now He is saying, "I want you to be more serious about loving me and allowing my love to flow through you." I know I personally need a more rigorous obedience to love, and a more energetic faith and trust in Him, hence this *Experiment of Prayer*.

As we move into this experience we know Satan will be more aggressive in all our lives, because his time is short. In the life of prayer, nothing annihilates answers to prayer as much as lovelessness in the heart of the intercessor.

What is Satan's easiest way to try to block the power of prayer in any prayer group? By violating the basic premise of Jesus' love commandments, through inner battles of "secret fault-finding," and through criticism of others, and even of ourselves.

The Sermon on the Mount says we are not to judge or criticize because it stops the flow of love, or the Holy Spirit who is love. *He is only released in love, through love, by love* (Eph 5:2) not by attempting to coerce God by our demanding others to change.

Our judgmental spirit prevents the movement of the Holy Spirit in our midst, and prevents the answers He longs to produce.

You might ask "Are you saying that my secret or open fault-finding attitudes are powerful enough to blackout God's response?" Yes, these attitudes create an atmosphere in which Jesus is hindered and any power in prayer is sabotaged. Satan is very much at work in any Christian gathering hoping to cancel out our love for one another and God's movement through the group (1 John 4:7–12, 20–21). What is canceled out is what the Scriptures call agreement or acceptance (Matt 18:19–20).

Agreement has many qualities. We list only a few:

- Identification or the ability to walk in another person's shoes (Matt 18:23–35).
- Patience with others (Eph 4:1–2).
- Discernment beyond flesh. Real discerning comes out of God's love. With God's love abandoned we merely "judge and criticize," thereby wounding the real person beyond the mask. A critical atmosphere is harmful to all concerned (Phil 1:9–11).

The amazing thing is that it takes only one critical person to weaken or even prevent the flow of love so the Holy Spirit cannot work. Any fault-finding is serious because it grieves the Holy Spirit (Eph 4:30–32). I have learned over the years that when my judging attitude has increased my level of God's love flowing through me has decreased.

Jesus means for your ability to love through Him to be stretched each time you come to prayer group. It is like "choir practice" each week. We practice love here in a relatively easy setting that we might be stretched and enabled to love with His love in more difficult settings.

Let us talk about this in more practical and detailed ways.

1. When I am irritated by another person in prayer, it shows me where I am. Something in me that is not what it ought to be has been triggered, or I would not be so irritated by something someone else has said (Matt 7:1–5).

2. When I am hurting in impatience, anger, pettiness of any kind, that tender place of fault-finding is where I need to grow. What I see in others, is showing in me.

   a. If I see self-centeredness, it is in me.

b. If I feel their self-love, it is also in me. This is often manifested in "self-display" as the saints have said.

c. If I see self-importance, it is in me.

d. If I see pride, it is in me.

e. Every negative aspect in another's personhood and prayer is in me. Content and length of prayer, control issues I hear and find fault with secretly, all are in me.

What are we to do when these ugly things surface in us?

First, repent while the prayer is still going on, adjust your thermostat of love quietly and privately, but adjust by confessing silently your judgment and criticism, your lack of love, which is sin.

Then, thank the Holy Spirit for revealing your sin, repent of it, accept forgiveness, get busy praying for the person or praying with the person and their prayer. *Enter in to their prayer totally and completely in nothing but love.* That is agreeing with another, or God's love in action. To enter into prayer, and be lifted above judgment is powerful and effective praying.

William Law was a contemporary of John Wesley. He was the author of *The Power of the Spirit,* formerly known as *A Serious Call to the Devout Life.* In this book he writes, "Divine Love is a new life and new nature and introduces you to a new world."[2] We must make the *choice* out of our will, to move in love!

Hannah Hurnard in her book, *The Winged Life*, wrote, "It's the reserves and the exceptions we insist on making to divine Love that brings failure. There must be no exceptions at all to God's call."[3]

2. Law, The *Power of the Spirit*, 122.
3. Hurnard, The *Winged Life*, 44.

1. If unloving thoughts are in our heart it changes the atmosphere. The person praying feels rejection, abandonment and loneliness. In prayer we are sensitized to other's feelings in a highly charged way. When we enter into criticism, those around us will feel let down because secret fault-finding is powerful and can be felt by others.

2. There is always something in every prayer we can agree with, so get back in order, get sin out of the center of your heart and mind—love.

3. We have often felt the power of God's love in this group, and the resulting faith which brings the answer (Gal 5:6). If we are in His love it will reveal His will (1 John 3:18–24).

Mary Welch, a devout woman of prayer, stated many times in the 1940's and 50's that "Love always lifts another and never adds to a person's burden."

God is calling us then to a quick accountability while we are here in this group on Tuesday night, that He might call us to a deeper accountability moment by moment. We know He is released, in ways we will never understand, through loving, believing prayer.

At the beginning, this Intercessory Prayer Group was focused on praying for ourselves, for others in the church at large, and the world itself. When the group was small years ago, we could bounce back and forth between personal and impersonal prayers easily.

Shortly after our first year we began to feel the urging of the Holy Spirit to more prayers for others and the world. Real answers began to come when we no longer prayed corporately so much for ourselves, but for others. Amazing results began to surface. The more we interceded for others, the more our own needs were met. The Book of Job gives us the pattern when it says, "And the Lord turned the captivity of Job when he prayed for his friends . . . also the Lord gave Job twice as much as he had before" (Job 42:10).

This focus on intercession for others continues to be our focus and thrust under the Holy Spirit. However, we do not want to ignore personal needs. A very Christ-like thing is evolving in that as personal needs may be expressed, the person praying or someone else will "multiply" or pray out over all people in that particular situation. In other words, our prayers are being magnified so that we pray not just for my church, my children, my world, but our church, our children and our world.

The Holy Spirit is sensitizing us to be as concerned for others as our own personal situation, and as a result, magnified prayers are more and more common in our group. That is the work of the Holy Spirit and very powerfully so.

The other side of the coin is that since we are all in more and more private prayer, our personal situations can be, yes, should be, handled as much as possible, with the Holy Spirit at home. When this is not possible, two or three of us gather to pray with someone in a more private setting. Any private request that comes forth on Tuesday night unexpectedly is prayed for in the group and then magnified for that situation globally.

In closing here are a few more "spiritual housekeeping" thoughts.

1. Since our group is so large, we generally request that each one pray aloud only one time, so others can pray aloud also. Keeping prayers short and focused is important. You will need to adjust this guideline to the size of your group.

2. Allow others to pray for concerns you feel concerned about. You are probably not the only person who feels that concern (Phil 2:3). Let each regard the other more important than herself/himself.

3. Avoid too much detail in your prayer—God knows all! The great saints of all the ages have taught that He is all wisdom so we do not have to inform Him. He is all knowledge so we do not have to instruct Him. He is all love so we do not have to persuade Him to do the loving thing.

4. Do not be afraid of silence, give others a chance to pray, do not jump in too soon, particularly if you have already prayed, but on the other hand do not leave the praying to a few people.

5. Ask the Holy Spirit to guide you!

6. Thank Him that you have a place to come and practice thinking only loving and kind thoughts. *That* is real prayer.

2

Asking, Seeking, Knocking Brings Answers

*And I say unto you, ask, and it shall be
given you; seek, and you shall find;
knock, and it shall be opened unto you.*
Luke 11:9

WE WILL go right to the heart of Jesus' words on the
mountain in this lesson. These are found in Matthew
7:1–13. Here Jesus lays out the profound necessity of bringing the thought life, or our interior life, into full alignment
with God's commandments. There must be no duplicity
within or without. When we live a life that is critical within
and sweet without we live by a double life. We are to feel
genuine love for others. There must be a profound integra-
tion of what we really believe and that is to take place in our
soul and spirit, and how we live it out.

We have spoken of how our prayers are canceled when
we are secretly fault-finding of others. Jesus, in this passage,
speaks of judgment as being so devastating to our prayer life
that it must be curtailed. The whole foundation for asking,
seeking, knocking must be built on no secret or open judgment and/or criticism of others.

What is it then to judge? What does it imply in our attitudes that is so defeating to God answering our prayers?

To judge means to assume God-like faculties which presume to measure another's motive, intent and conduct. To judge means I become a judge or evaluator of another's life and conduct. We must never loose sight of the fact that as mortals we do not know all that is in another person's heart. We must ask why he is what he is, and why he does what he does. When I assume God-like qualities, and measure another person's motive, I am forgetting my place as a sinner and human being. I have claimed for myself great arrogance and pride in trying to be like God Himself. I am to leave that presumption and evaluation to God. Even He is leaving the final assessing to the last and final Day of Judgment (John 5:22). Even God is not judging anyone now, not even you or me, and the Scriptures say Jesus is also not judging anyone now (John 8:15).

Instead of using energy to enter God's realm of evaluator, in which I am totally inept anyway, use this energy to ask, seek and knock. I cannot even properly "judge" myself because I am often too harsh on myself or too easy on myself. This energy is to be used to ask, seek, and knock on behalf of those who are a thorn in my side: asking, seeking, knocking that their needs will be met and that they will be all God wants them to be. Our prayers, using this energy, are lifted into different realms of cleansing for all concerned.

A study of the passages containing the three words "asking, seeking, knocking" reveals that Jesus highlights the fact that this is an important issue of persisting in prayer. The first such passage is Matthew 7:7, but so crucial is the need for persistence or importunity that Jesus mentions it again in the settings of Luke 11:1–13 and Luke 18:1–8.

Jesus is saying in Luke 11:1–3 that God is not like the judge or friend, both of whom had to have their resistance broken down by unwavering demands on them. Rather, Jesus is more than willing to give good gifts to them that ask Him (Matt 7:9–11). If evil men love to give good gifts to their children, how much more does our loving Father yearn to give the most precious gift of all to His children, the priceless gift of the Holy Spirit, to them who ask Him (Luke 11:13).

In other words, all asking, seeking, knocking aims toward the releasing of the Holy Spirit in the midst of the problem, as the gift that is needed. Andrew Murray states, "The love of God is the Holy Spirit" (Romans 5:5). Prayer, persistent prayer, begins to release the Presence of the Holy Spirit in our midst. The releasing of God's love and power, the releasing of the Solution, Jesus Himself, as the Holy Spirit (2 Cor 3:17) is God's greatest answer to prayer. He literally comes Himself in the form of the Holy Spirit. Whenever He is released, the answer has come! His greatest gift is Himself, the only gift that really satisfies and fulfills us!

Asking, seeking, knocking persistently demands time and energy. There are several reasons for this.

1. In praying-through the many possibilities and so-lutions, we might be projecting on God to bring about our own will and way.

2. He begins to work through us a deeper desire for His way and His timing, no matter what it takes.

3. We begin to see the Holy Spirit alone can solve the situation, and we passionately desire His coming (Jer 29:13).

4. When we truly want Him more than anything, He comes!

In ways we do not understand, He has been working in us as we persist in prayer—bringing us to the end of our selves, changing our attitudes and motives, and humbling us to submit to Jesus' way of doing things. John 16:7–13 says that He convicts us of our sins, of righteousness and judgment.

In ways we do not realize at the time, as we persist in prayer, He moves increasingly in our lives, taking more dominion and leadership, plus revealing Himself to us to a greater extent.

Luke 11:14–26 says that as we ask, seek and knock, the Holy Spirit begins to show us that we must bind the strong man, Satan, or push him back so a stronger man, Jesus, can attack him and overpower him, taking away Satan's power.

The strong man, Satan, can only be bound and rendered helpless when the Holy Spirit is released through much asking, seeking, knocking. Strong, persistent prayer of the Holy Spirit (Rom 8:26) releases in us, through asking, seeking, knocking, God's power to overcome Satan and his stronghold of deception. The Holy Spirit is now free to minister to the person and the situation.

Basilea Schlinck makes clear in a very compelling way that persistent intercession pushes Satan back and frees people so they can respond to the Holy Spirit's wooing to do right. Only this manner of prayer rebuffs Satan. This type of prayer is costly to us (Mark 9:14–29) as we come against Satan (1 Pet 5:8–9; Eph 6:10–18). We persist in prayer to keep evil out of a situation. The old adage says, "What is gained by prayer must be maintained by prayer." So in Luke 11:1–13 we see persistent prayer releasing the Holy Spirit, and the Holy Spirit defeating Satan.

In the Luke 18:1–8 passage we see evidence of another consequence of asking, seeking, knocking. Jesus says in verses 7–8 that God will assuredly bring about justice for His elect. He hears their crying out day and night. He will not ignore their persistence, we can depend on that! His concern is whether or not we are learning a deepening faith and trust in Him. After all, faith is what brings the answer, not just saying the words of the prayer. Victory is brought about through faith and trust in Him and His Word (1 John 5:4). Faith is the victory through prayer.

Asking, seeking, knocking brings us into a deepening relationship with Jesus. We know Him better, we spend time together, we see answers to other prayers coming forth, and we have more confidence in Him as we see Him working in lives.

My mother used to talk about "untroubled trust." Such trust comes out of a deep-rooted knowing of Jesus. Faith in Him is the thing God is looking for (Heb 11:6), and our expectant faith releases the answer. *Faith* is the victory (Mark 11:20–24).

We know it is foretold that when Jesus comes He will find little faith in the earth (Matt 24:10–13). Anyone who is seriously persevering in prayer—asking, seeking, knocking—will find the Holy Spirit revealing Jesus (John 15:26). As we see Him as our friend and teacher, we will grow in faith by leaps and bounds, because we are in a growing, friendly relationship with Him.

I find it interesting that Luke 18:9–14 talks about the humility that is necessary to be heard by God. In asking, seeking, knocking, the more we touch the Reality of Jesus, and have faith in Him, the less we have confidence in ourselves, and enter a new humility or lack of self-sufficiency and self-reliance. Our dependency deepens as we trust Him more. Probably we could say the bedrock of asking, seeking, knocking is the deepening friendship with the Holy Spirit, which bring us to a laying down of our concerns and our life, and becoming more and more concerned over God's concerns: His Kingdom coming, His will being done here as in Heaven, and His life flowing through us more and more. We decrease and He increases! What a powerful experience it is to ask, to seek, to knock.

In verse 8 of Matthew 7, Jesus is reaffirming again that if we ask, seek, knock, He *will* answer us. Everyone who asks, *receives*, he who seeks *finds*, he who knocks, *to him it shall be opened*. But we believe Jesus is saying we need to be sure our asking, seeking, knocking is built on not judging anyone in the situation for whom you are praying.

There is another profound law involved here—the power of sowing and reaping. It is found in verse 2 of Matthew 7, "for in the way you judge, you will be judged, and by your standard of measure it will be measured to you."

We set in motion a terrible chain reaction when we judge. What we give out, we get back—or the law of "sowing and reaping," as found in Galatians 6:7–9, "whatever a man sows, that he also reaps."

If I judge in bitterness and anger, with no mercy toward the other person, I will be judged in the very same bitter and angry way. I perpetuate an attitude, whether good or evil, when I judge. Jesus is saying, "Stop the cycle of darkness, by beginning to pray for the other person, so what we give out is love, which finds expression in asking, seeking, knocking." Then, as we give out love, we get love back.

It is a frightening commandment, but one that is fixed in God's laws. It's such joy to sow love, because that will come back to us. But what pain to sow resentment and receive resentment in return!

The law of sowing and reaping is taught forcibly in Matthew 7. Jesus says in Matthew 7:1–2 that what you give out will back to you. If I am critical, it will come back to me. The measure or intensity of my judging someone else comes back in the same degree of intensity to me and to you.

Jesus is saying that this cycle of returning evil for evil must be broken, and it is broken in our prayer life as the Holy Spirit teaches us the power of ceasing all judgment and criticism. James chapter 3 speaks of the power of the tongue and the evil destruction it can produce. Only God's love can break the cycle of destruction, evil for evil. Through prayer God's love is manifest in the situation, rather than judgment, which cancels God's love.

An amazing reality begins to emerge, says Jesus in this passage of Matthew 7:9–11. The more we refrain from god-like judgment of others, and use that energy to ask, seek and knock, the more He begins to move us into a glorious new place in Him. I begin to see His changes in me, and those for whom I pray. His goodness, His loving kindness, His great mercies begin to pervade my relationship with Him. In new ways He floods my thoughts and heart with a deepening reality that *He is good.* He does all things well. His precepts concerning everything are righteous and good. He yearns to bless us with great, eternal goodness (Ps 31:19–24).

He begins to show me the power of His love that is released when I obey His commandment not to judge, but pray. In spite of my puny attempts and frequent failure, the joy of experiencing His power and His faithfulness is amazing. He honors me because He knows my heart is fixed on obeying this very vital commandment to judge not. Praise His Name!

Out of this growing reality of His loving kindness and total faithfulness, by praying for these people who hurt or offend me, I am brought into the reality of how much He wants to give good gifts to those who ask (Matt 7:7–11). These good gifts are released only through love, not judgment. The more we pray for those who persecute us the more the atmosphere of Jesus presses in on us to love constantly, whether in or out of prayer, so we learn to stay in His love, not judgment. He lifts us up into a new realm of wanting to see Him give good gifts, rather than nursing or coddling a wrong or injustice through feeding on judgment and criticism.

As He is cleansing us of our wrong thinking and acting, He places Christ-like love in our hearts for those who persecute us. Gradually the attitude of Jesus toward them becomes our attitude whether we are in or out of our prayer time.

It is easy for there to be inconsistency in us. We can have Jesus' attitude toward them while in prayer, but when we leave the prayer place we slip back into a fleshly human response. Jesus is saying, "Persevere until your attitude toward them is changed and more constant." This comes about only through *much prayer*, but we will see much answered prayer if we allow Jesus to do a perfect or maturing work in us as He changes us in our times of prayer. Oh, that His love might flow through us all the time.

He causes us to treat them as Jesus would treat them. Or we could say, to treat them as God treats us with compassion, love, forgiveness and great patience. Of course this is the unfolding of the Golden Rule (Matt 7:12). Treat others as you have prayed for them. Treat them as you would want them to treat you. Stay in the love you found in prayer as you move in your contact with them (Jas 2:8–9). Allow His God-life, which is love, to flow through you to them. It will come as night follows day, if we ask, seek and knock. We allow time for Him to change our attitudes into His attitudes. How exciting! Asking, seeking, knocking brings us into Divine love for them and allows us to be channels for God's love.

A transformation begins to takes place in us. Our prayer time becomes a place of transformation into Jesus' image and He takes dominion over our thought life more and more. All becomes prayer; all becomes responsiveness to His love. It is life changing when we are allowing Him to empower us to not judge, but pray. We begin to see results totally impossible through judgment and criticism. God's great, loving creativity and abundance begins to flow through us out to others. He gives to them what He has given to us. To be His channels of love and grace is life's great fulfillment! It produces miracles of His love.

Finally, His wisdom comes to us—when to speak, when not to speak; when it is in His will to share and when it would be very unwise. Jesus said, "Only those with eyes to see, ears to hear, can truly receive" (Mark 8:18). We learn when to give our pearls and when to refrain. His wisdom becomes our wisdom.

You may say to me, "But what if we see or experience a person doing real wrong, clearly and unmistakably? What is the difference between righteous discernment and the fatal judgmental attitude?"

The passage in Matthew 7:3–5 says, "Be sure you are dealing with the log in your own eye before you attack the speck in the other's eye." Even if I see actual wrong, I am also "wrong" if I am out of God's compassionate love. Paul says the only way to properly speak any criticism is with weeping, in great love, for the other person (Phil 3:18). Only real discernment comes out of deep love. Often what we call discernment is only a license to be judgmental. When there is no prayer over this episode, we become just as guilty as the offender. In prayer, the Holy Spirit shows us how much of a log is in our eye. The tendency to do the very same thing that has been done to us lives in us. We marvel not at the other person but at ourselves and our desire and ability to "save our own neck" at whatever the cost. I do not know who first said this, but it is powerfully true, "Given the right opportunity, there is no telling what we would do if it were not for Jesus in our hearts." If we are serious about this matter we see that we too probably could not have done as well as the other person, given their set of circumstances.

We begin to really see what is in us in the prayer life. We become well acquainted with the log of sin in us and treat with growing compassion the speck in our brother's eye. Our own weaknesses and sins deeply unite us with all other sinners. We are all "cut off the same piece of cloth."

- Will you stay out of God-like judgments toward others? Will you use that energy to ask, seek and knock on their behalf?

- Will you treat them out of your prayer attitudes of touching God's love and not out of judgmental prayerless attitudes?

- Will you stay with the Holy Spirit until He wells up within you in love and compassion? Will you allow Him to really show you yourself and then take responsibility for your part, not blaming others?

- Will you allow Him to so flood the entire situation in His healing love that you are changed more into His image?

May He have more dominion over your thought life and love life. May we live out of Matthew 7:1–14 this week.

3

The Power of Secrecy

That thine alms may be in secret . . .
and thy Father which seeth in secret
Himself shall reward thee openly.
Matthew 6:4

But thou, when thou prayest, enter into thy closet,
and when thou has shut thy door, pray to thy
Father which is in secret; and thy Father which
seeth in secret shall reward thee openly.
Matthew 6:6

That thou appear not unto men to fast,
but into thy Father which is in secret . . .
and thy Father, which seeth in secret,
shall reward thee openly.
Matthew 6:18

THE GREAT prayer movement of the 1930's–60's called *The Camps Farthest Out* was founded by Dr. Glenn Clark in the 1930's. It was my great privilege to hear Dr. Clark teach many times. He loved the topic of the great spiritual laws contained in this chapter. The first spiritual law is: "The more invisible a thing is, the more powerful it is," or we could say, "The more secret and hidden prayer is, the more powerful it is."[1] Jesus states this spiritual concept pertaining to three separate areas in Matthew chapter 6.

He begins with the realm of giving when He states "do not let your left hand know what the right is doing." Do not broadcast to anyone what you are giving or even let one hand know what the other hand is doing! That is utter secrecy indeed (Matt 6:1–4)! In other words, recognition or applause from others can puff us up.

Secondly, Jesus applies it also to our fasting (Matt 6:16–18). We should not seek to be praised or lifted up by others because of results from prayer that truly costs us something in sacrificing such things as food, time, or sleep.

Our praying community has learned the hard lesson regarding fasting prayer. We have come to realize that we must be careful so that we are not trying to force God to our way of thinking nor seeking to control Him. Rather, fasting is saying we desire Him, His will and way of doing things beyond desiring food, rest, pleasure or comfort of any kind.

The third area of "the more invisible, the more powerful" is in the closet or room where we talk with God daily. Jesus says that Father so enjoys the solitary person shut into the place of private prayer because He has that person all to Himself, and the individual has God all to himself—focused, intent, sincere, *alone with Him.*

A life changing friendship of closeness begins to spring up. We honor and reverence God when we seek Him alone and He loves to honor us before others (Matt 6:5–6). One person has said, "God loves doing His business in small out of the way, private places because God moves in great mystery and great unknowingness."

The great saints all speak of "Divine Hidings," even as God commanded Elijah to hide by the brook Cherith

1. Clark, *The Lord's Prayer*, p. 27.

so he might be fed with God's word and drink the waters of the Holy Spirit. He needed to be tucked away under the shadow of the Almighty, safe from others, himself, his ego and pride—all pressure and visibility removed. What a relief to not have to perform or to measure up, only to "be" with God.

Verse 5 of I Kings 17 says, "He went and dwelt there." You and I too must learn to go into our place of prayer or hide away where we intimately learn to live and dwell with God Himself.

4

Our Wants or What We Need

*But when you pray, use not vain repetitions as
the heathens do . . . for they think that they shall be
heard for their much speaking. Be not ye therefore
like unto them . . . for your Father knoweth what
things ye have need of, before ye ask Him.*
Matthew 6:7–8

JESUS GIVES two statements of guidance about how to
avoid a serious pitfall in what we are to say to God in
solitude and in public:

1. First, we are to avoid praying in long and lengthy
   prayers as if to overwhelm and coerce God to do
   what we expect of Him—to convince Him that
   what we want must indeed be right and He must
   do as we want! Secondly, we are to avoid vain
   repetitions or phrases which we really do not understand in any meaningful way—praying what is
   rote and not from the heart. The saints have all said
   prayer from the lips and not the heart is insincere.
   God wants "heart prayer."

2. Father knows exactly what we need, and what we
   need is often far from what we want (v. 8). A resistance exists in all of us that does not want to
   face what we truly need God to do in us. True
   prayer allows the Holy Spirit to begin to change

our asking, seeking, knocking to be more in alignment with God's will. What an amazing process!
We pray our wants until the Holy Spirit begins
to help us finally pray out of our needs, and what
is more in God's will, which is our highest good.
There is nothing anymore exciting than to hear the
"still small voice" gently suggesting the *real truth*
to pray! What a thrilling journey because we speak
to a living Lord!

Are there times when you are in your "cloistered closet"
so busy telling God what to do and when to do it, you cannot hear His voice? May you and I listen to His response to
what we have prayed so we do not ask amiss (Jas 4:3).

My mother was wonderful in laying out to God what
she felt about a circumstance in prayer. When she was finished pouring out her opinion about what needed to be
done, she would say, "Father, this is my opinion, what is
your divine opinion about what I have just said?" Then she
would listen for Him to speak to her about His response.
This did not always come immediately. She knew what it
meant to wait for the answer. This theme will be developed
in more depth in a later chapter.

He loves us too much to do anything that would be
the least barrier to the highest and best for us. Will you allow Him to bring your true condition to the light? He will
do all that is best for you. He will bring into fruition that
which will help and bless you the most.

5

Do We Say or Pray the Lords Prayer?

After this manner pray ye: . . .
Matthew 6:9

IT WOULD be hard to believe that any one seeking to share insights of our beloved Lord's pattern for prayer ever approaches it without wonder and awe, feeling totally inadequate, to enter it's depths of adoration, petition, and contrition. In such astonishing brevity and conciseness, every facet of our prayer life is unfolded and the "highway of our Lord" is opened up to us.

Jean Nicholas Grou (1730–1803), one of the greatest men writing on the prayer life of another day has this to say about the Lord's Prayer.

"Matthew 6:9 after this manner pray ye:

- The Lord's Prayer is holy ground given to us by Jesus Christ Himself to suit His own purposes, and not ours.

- You shall regulate your lives according to this prayer. This prayer is the most perfect rule of conduct we can have.

- It is the summary of the gospel, the very essence of all that is most perfect in the moral and spiritual teaching of Jesus Christ.

- Do we think, speak, and act in conformity with this prayer?
- Is the Lord's Prayer what I truly think, truly feel, what I truly desire?
- This prayer has always been placed above all others. A Christian can say nothing in praise of God or ask Him for anything which is not contained in it.
- It is the prayer of the heart.
- Only the Holy Ghost can inspire the depth of this prayer."[1]

It is my heart felt belief that the Lord's Prayer needs to be prayed *very slowly*, giving the person praying these words time to ponder, to reflect, to truly pray the words.

As we study this eternal prayer, will you ask the Spirit of God to help you, from the heart, prayerfully pray slowly and reverently? Our praying community when studying The Lord's Prayer, prayed it phrase by phrase with much silence after each statement. It was very powerful! Will you take some time now at the end of this chapter to slowly and meaningfully pray these phrases?

1. Grou, *How To Pray*, 101–4.

6

Knowing Him as Father

Our Father, who art in Heaven.
Matthew 6:9

To BEGIN this chapter I want to focus on the word "our." The interconnectedness of humanity is staggering to our natural minds. Each person you meet either is your brother or sister in Jesus Christ, or a potential brother or sister in Jesus Christ.

In John 13:34–35 Jesus says, "We are to love others, as I have loved you." When we come to the alter of God in prayer our heart must be able to receive God's own holy love. The lowest level of God's love is good will or loving kindness toward everyone. It is the dear Holy Spirit who thus empowers us to treat all appropriately. This is the starting point in obeying the words found in John 13:34 in which Jesus says, "a new commandment I give unto you, that you love one another as I have loved you."

We cannot exclude anyone when we say "our." To withhold God's love from flowing through us to anyone is very grievous to the Holy Spirit. The following represents a short list of possibilities of who we cannot exclude:

- The person hardest for us to love.
- Our worst enemy.
- The person you do not like.
- People who do not do what we want them to do.

- People radically different from us.
- The worst sinner.
- Every evil leader in the world.

We know that in our flesh, with human love, this is totally impossible! Only the precious indwelling Holy Spirit can give us, not only once, but repeatedly the infilling of the love of God (Rom 5:5) we all so desperately need for others and our self.

This supernatural experience of receiving love for our self and other's happens at the altar of daily prayer. He will allow us to see our lovelessness, our self-centeredness, our self-assertiveness, until we cry out to Him from the depths of our heart, to come to us and impart His holy love—*to set our wills* to treat all with respect, kindness, and goodwill.

One of the greatest things in my prayer life is that the Holy Spirit reveals to me that my will must lead my emotions. The setting or empowering the will to do right in spite of everything is the seat of our spirituality, not our emotions. Only in secret lingering time with Father, Son and Holy Spirit can we be changed to become more like Him, and allow His love to flow through us.

One of the members of our praying community, by the power of the Holy Spirit, had allowed Him to set his will to do right concerning a member of our group whom he did not care for at all. After several years of acting out of his will in loving actions, while they stood talking in the parking lot of the church after the prayer group met, he was literally flooded with God's love for this person. Not only a determination of the will, but his whole being was washed over again and again by God's pure holy love. No words can ever adequately say how glorious it is! He had been doing the loving kind thing and now God gave Him the emotional reality as well.

Is there anyone you have shut out of God's love flowing through you to them? It is a serious offense to the Holy Spirit, the Love of God, to refuse love to anyone at all. Invite the Holy Spirit to cleanse you and set your will, not your emotions, to love others. Meet them in loving, kind, and caring ways. Then you will do right no matter what the emotions say. At the appointed time He will flood you with great joy and love.

7

The Holy Spirit Reveals
Father's Love

Our Father which art in Heaven . . .
Matthew 6:9

THE WORD "Father" is a subject that today is clothed in painful contexts in many men's and women's lives. In other's lives, it is a word of comfort and strength. To many the word spoken by their earthly father had no reliability or truth. While to others, the father's word was something on which they could depend. In both situations our relationship with our earthly father has impacted us.

I can remember waiting for a ride one chilly late November evening at the College of Music in Cincinnati, Ohio. I had finished my piano lesson and I was waiting for Daddy to drive by the College to give me a ride home. First, he was going to meet my grandmother who was arriving from Wichita, Kansas at the Union Station. I was barely 14 years old and felt very grown up. At first I stood inside the door of the College, but as time continued to pass I went outside and sat on the steps. The darkness settled down over the city, the air now had a definite chill to it, and faculty members would brush by me and say things such as,

"Have they forgotten to come get you?"

"No sir, I am waiting on my Daddy." I would reply.

"Will you be alright out here? It's so dark."

"Yes, my Daddy is coming to get me," was my reply.

"Don't let anyone get you!"

"No sir, my Daddy is coming; he's just a little late that's all."

I *was* getting a little afraid as the streets and sidewalks were thinning out of people. But, I reassured myself that Daddy had never forgotten to pick me up and today was going to be no different.

Suddenly, after sitting there, what I thought to be an eternity, I saw our old green Buick coming up the street. Then, it was at the corner and making the turn at the steps. I was so overjoyed, so relieved, so thrilled that my expectations of Daddy's reliability were again true. I leaped off the steps and ran toward the car. Such love for my Daddy welled up in me. He came, He came! What a precious sight to see him get out of the car and come to hug me. The train had been delayed, but my Daddy came!

That same welling up of love and thanksgiving is what our Heavenly Father wants us to feel for Him in a close and loved way. There is an often overlooked verse about the Holy Spirit's mission of causing us to be knowingly connected to Him as Father, "Because you are sons and daughters, God has sent forth the Spirit of His Son into your heart's crying Abba, Father" (Gal 4:6).

In other words, the indwelling Holy Spirit is to bring about a supernatural connection between God and you so you have a sense of sonship or daughtership that causes you to love Him and know Him as Daddy. This sense of adoption grows all our lifetime as we meet Him daily in prayer. Our concept of God and Father is changed as we meet Him daily. We see new vistas of His rich and loving Fatherhood as we meet Him over and over again in daily prayer.

Have you ever sat quietly in your prayer time and asked the Holy Spirit to cause you to experience and know in your human spirit that God is truly your Father? That

He can be counted on? He so wants you to know Him as Abba, Daddy.

Though He is transcendent, invisible, ruling and reigning on His throne in the third Heaven—you will be connected to Him in mysterious and life altering ways. He longs to have you know in your deepest self His Fatherly connection to you.

Stop right now and ask the Spirit of Jesus to give you a greater assurance of that eternal connection. Our Father, which art in Heaven . . .

8

Treasure God's Name

. . . hallowed be Thy name
Matthew 6:9c

THE WORD "hallowed" is not commonly used today, so it sounds strange and foreign to us. However, the many rich shades of the word, when applied to God, enhance the descriptive power of the word "hallowed." Hallowed means we are to honor, treasure, and cherish the profound name of God the Father, God the Son, and God the Holy Spirit.

The hallowing of God's name as Father, Son and Holy Spirit is not to be an intellectual concept only, but a burning Reality in our heart, and soul. The experiential truth of this heavenly attitude begins to be birthed in us as we enter daily the Holy of Holies—our inner heart sanctuary. Cloistered away from all human disturbances in one's prayer closet, He is allowed an opportunity to unveil Himself to us as we wait and meditate on His Word (2 Cor 3:18).

In the wonders of this Divine/human exchange, our deepest eternal self begins to open as a flower, ever so slowly to His pure and wondrous Presence. The precious Holy Spirit begins to fan the flame of God's love for us (Rom 5:5) and we timidly and with caution begin to actually receive the Presence of Jesus. Our attention begins to be more and more captivated by Him. He wants to perfect our receptivity so it becomes highly sensitive to Him, and totally open to receiving Him.

We have in reality been seeking our whole life for these times with Father, Son, and Holy Spirit. Our entire being craves for what only He can give. No greater experience exists in all of life than experientially knowing God. Out of these encounters we begin to love Him and be comfortable with Him. Our spiritual autobiography begins.

Only the blessed Holy Spirit can enable us to confront God and our deepest self. As this Presence continues the Spirit of Faith (2 Cor 4:13), the Holy Spirit strengthens us to not only come to Jesus and Father, but He is the one who helps us to trust Father, Son, and Holy Spirit. He also gives us a much needed courage to continue on this way.

This is the ongoingness of the prayer life, daily, weekly, monthly and year by year—to *ever go deeper into the Sacred Presence—ever deeper into the wonder of His name and nature.* The life changing result of daily coming is beyond description! The unfolding of God's life in us is a true miracle! We begin to love Him more and more dearly and receive His love more totally.

How much of God do you truly want? How much of God are you able to receive? How much of your time are you willing to give to seeking and knowing Him? Your cherishing of His name is in direct measure to your living in His Holy Presence.

Jesus in the Gospel of John (14:10) so honored and hallowed Father's name that He says, "the Father that dwells in Me, He does the works." May you and I so worship and cherish Father, Son and Holy Spirit, in all areas of our life that we might be totally given to God. This will allow Him to do His works in and through us according to His calling in our life.

Will you allow the Holy Spirit to consecrate your life around all Jesus is? To unfold the image and nature of Jesus as you are able to receive Him? Not only in your intentional time daily, but to humbly lift Him up in adoration and worship all through your day.

9

Are You Living in the Kingdom Now?

*Thy Kingdom come, Thy will be done
in earth, as it is in Heaven.*
Matthew 6:10

I HAVE spoken of the *Camps Farthest Out*, and what a great privilege it was to be a part of that prayer movement. Another great central theme that I learned was that each one of us was to live in the Kingdom of God, *now, today.* We were also taught that the Holy Spirit is our Helper to reveal Jesus to us, (John 15:26) and enables us to live in the Kingdom with the King by drawing on Jesus' life in us (John 16:13–15).

There were certain questions we were to ask our self from Glenn Clark's teaching on the Kingdom:

1. Are we living in the Kingdom of God now? If not, why not, and what hinders you?

2. Are you under the King's authority? If not, at what point are you not submitted to His authority?

3. Are you living in obedience to Kingdom rules? Do you know the rules of the Kingdom from His word?

4. Are you in close relationship to the indwelling Holy Spirit, so you can receive empowerment

from Him to stay in God's love toward everyone? Are you acting righteously and in peace toward all? Are you experiencing joy over knowing Him? (Rom 14:17)

5. Living in the Kingdom of God means you are staying close to Father, Son, and Holy Spirit. Are you staying in God's Presence throughout the day? (Acts 17:28)

6. Are you seeking out of your will, not the emotions, to stay close to Father, Son, and Holy Spirit, in a vital obedience?

7. Is the atmosphere of the Kingdom, which brings Heaven down to earth, making a difference in the environment wherever you are?

Glenn Clark would say, "If you are living in the Kingdom of God you are with the right person at the right time and in the right place. This sense of rightness brings an awareness of a Heavenly reality of moving through the day being exactly where He wants you to be."[1]

What did Jesus say about the Kingdom of God?

1. "And when He was demanded of the Pharisees when the Kingdom of God should come He answered them and said, 'The Kingdom of God comes not by observation: Neither shall they say, "Lo here" or "lo there," for behold the Kingdom of Heaven is within you'" (Luke 17:20–21). St. Teresa of Avila said, "The inward reality of the King taking up residency in our hearts is that we might rejoice in His occupancy and come to Him."[2]

1. In my many conversations with Dr. Clark over 10 years he would often make these statements.

2. I have discovered this quote in my reading but am not able to locate the source.

2. The Holy Spirit imparts to us Jesus' righteousness, peace, and joy in and through the Indwelling Spirit (Rom 14:17). He flows in us and through us as we commune with Him. This is how the Kingdom is manifested now.

3. What is our part in bringing in the Kingdom of God? Scriptures teach that we are to take the humble way. Through humility the Kingdom of God is allowed expression.

   a. The two parables found in Luke 13:18–21 speak of humble duties—taking the way of modesty and lowliness—a humble grain, a mustard seed, planted in a field bringing forth a great tree—shade, comfort, loveliness to birds and human life. We are to go about our praying no matter how common our tasks, allowing God to flow through us in our most ordinary days. He will bring forth fruit.

   b. Secondly, it is like leaven which a woman hid in three measures of meal, till the whole loaf was leavened. Our life is infused in His life through prayer and His word which allows His life to bless everyone we meet. Our prayer life goes to the end of the earth as we intercede round the world.

   c. The third way the kingdom is allowed access is through the heart yearning prayers of the Holy Spirit welling up in our times of prayer. In all my life I have never experienced any more powerful reality of these verses than in the last few years. A longing so overwhelming, so passionately powerful, so wistfully crying out for God's Kingdom to come to this broken world. Truly the entire creation is in pain even as we groan within ourselves for Jesus to come and set up His Kingdom here (Rom 8:16–23). At times in prayer we are nearly overcome with yearning for Jesus to come! These inexpressible, but powerful prayers are a means of praying in the Kingdom. It is the Holy Spirit longing for Jesus to set up His Kingship here.

May we be faithful to our King Jesus that His life might flow through His people unhindered and pure, that we will see the Kingdom of our Lord and of His Christ as He reigns forever and forever (Rev 11:15).

10

Making His Will Our Will

Thy Will be done on earth as it is in Heaven.
Matthew 6:10

M AKING HIS will our will certainly is a life time journey.
It is with difficulty that we begin to talk about wanting God's will in this realm as totally as it is experienced in the Heavenly Realm because it is my tendency to do what I feel is right to do. However, in the prayer closet, we begin to love Him so deeply that we yearn to do His will.

There are no words to express how the precious Holy Spirit is brooding over our will to bring it into total alignment with His will! He wants us to be so open to the still small voice of the Spirit of God in us that we yield ourselves completely to His desires. ". . . A vessel unto honor, sanctified and meet, for the Master's use, and prepared unto every good work" (2 Tim 2:21).

What an extraordinary prayer progression this is, day by day, week by week, month by month, year by year, in the secret place, often wrestling with God, but allowing Him to bring our stubborn rebellious will into union with His will (Gen 32:24–32)!

I understand the giving of our self in a once in a lifetime unconditional surrender. After a year and a half of seeking the Holy Spirit and making restitution of all my sin and errors, He came in great authority and flooded my life with Jesus. I surrendered as completely as I knew how, whereas before I had fought and resisted yielding my will totally.

I was in my early 40's when the Holy Spirit empowered me and ushered in a whole new world and reality of Jesus (John 16:13–15). Though I was surrendered as completely as I knew how to be, I found however, it is in *daily extensive times with God* that the Holy Spirit continues to reveal the deep, hidden underground chambers of resistance to God. The entitlement of the self-life manifests itself in motives, attitudes, and desires that I must continually relinquish to Him.

Sometimes as the Holy Spirit uncovers and surfaces such darkness it can be most painful, but as we go along with Him we are enabled by the Holy Spirit to face our self many times in the light and love of our precious Lord. These experiences are such a sacred and humble time to let go, repent, and to find Jesus' Presence ever increasingly comforting. We begin to know Him to be truly more intimately dear as He brings our will and His will into harmony and peace.

I hunger to pray, "Thy will be done on earth even as it is done in Heaven" with as much heart truthfulness and genuineness as Jesus prayed this same prayer, "not My will, but Thine be done" (Luke 22:42–43). To know Him ever more fully and truly yielding our self-will to Him—our wills in union—there is no greater human experience.

Are you allowing the indwelling Holy Spirit to draw you more into His likeness, of desiring one will with God the Father, God the Son, God the Holy Spirit? This emerges as we spend time with Him being transparent and more authentic. Are we willing to change and cry out to the Holy Spirit to have His way with us *now today*?

11

He Is the Supplier of Our Needs

Give us this day our daily bread
Matthew 6:11

A VERY surprising experience begins to slowly unfold in
our prayer chamber. We begin to be more conscious of
our sins against God and others, our faults and our personal
issues begin to be surfaced from within the highly protected
citadel of our selfhood. The precious Holy Spirit allows us
to see our self-centeredness, our insecurities, anger, wound-
edness, and pride. Our modes of survival and coping are
visible to us and dismantled brick by brick before our very
eyes, as we yield to His way.

A whole new awareness of our inability to change
our self, our powerlessness to control God and others, our
facade of what we have sought to build into our selfhood,
is being slowly altered by the Indwelling Holy Spirit, who
brings the truth to us (John 14:26) and most importantly,
begins to flood us with God's love for us (Rom 5:5).

What a transforming experience to begin to experience God's eternal love for us. Our insulations that have
stood for years against Him and our protective mask of the
self-life melt away as we *know He Loves us just as we are*
forlorn, hurting, needy and frightened. "While we were yet
sinners, Christ died for us" (Rom 5:8).

What a blessed relief to stop all pretending, all masking of our true feelings and simply to "*be*" with Him, facing our inner turmoil and unrest. To allow Him to minister to us out of His unconditional love, we can dare to be real, honest, confessional, and repentant. We can dare to make restitution with those we have sinned against in word and deed. What unspeakable relief! He wants to be all we need and empower us to allow Him to be truly our friend (John 15:14–15).

We had thought it all depended on us. We thought our job and paycheck was our responsibility alone. We had to be responsible for meeting all our needs, but in the prayer closet, He begins to unfold His love as a "caring for us" love. He has given us our job, He is our source of money, He gives us strength to work and be responsible, but we are removed from "being in charge," because "He is in charge" (Matt 6:33).

I believe it is a theme of Martin Luther that teaches God will start a revolution in you if you will meet Him daily. That revolution brings us into the reality of our profound weakness—crying out to Him "Father, give me what I need today." Whatever the need may be, daily physical bread or daily spiritual bread, we turn to Him, no longer to our meager inadequate resources (2 Cor 12:9–10). Jesus said we are to ask, seek and knock for all we need. Allowing Father to be our source in all things from bread to life work, all is from Him and done in Him through His loving Holy Spirit.

He loves to hear His children ask and He loves to respond to the need. Are you talking everything over with Him? Are you relying on Him? Are you able to receive from Him? Do you trust Him to meet your daily needs? May the secret place of prayer be indeed Holy Ground!

12

As He Forgives Us We Forgive

Forgive us our debts as we forgive our debtor's.
Matthew 6:12

*For if you forgive men their trespasses your
Heavenly Father will also forgive you: but if you
forgive not men their trespasses neither will
your Father forgive your trespasses.*
Matthew 6:14–15

OVER MANY years, men and women in our praying
community have had numerous opportunities to experience the amazing Presence of the Holy Spirit pouring
out God's love for them, thereby receiving His forgiving
love to forgive others. Just recently one of the men had a
glorious experience in releasing the joy and wonder of God's
reconciliation love in a serious longstanding bitterness.

This man did not even realize the depth of his unforgiveness toward two of his co-workers, who had been
treating him for sometime, in an angry and unforgiving
way. Out of their animosity over the handling of a situation
they quite literally chose to ignore their part and blame
him for everything. Hostility had taken over on both sides
(Matt 5:38). An eye for an eye, a tooth for a tooth ruled
the situation, which was growing steadily worse. Nothing
so cuts off God's redeeming love and power as this "talionic

47

impulse" of doing back to the other person exactly what they have done to us.

One day as this man was meditating in God's word, and waiting on God, the Holy Spirit spoke to him. "Your unforgiveness toward these two men has caused you to act just as they are acting. They have brought you down to their level. You have grieved Me, as you have not once cried out to Me to help you. You have cancelled out God's love flowing through you to them. I want you to repent of this action" (Eph 4:30, Rom 5:5).

He was so stricken and convicted that tears began to roll down his face. He cried out, "Lord Jesus, I do repent, forgive me, cleanse me by Your precious Blood." Even as he was crying out, our Beloved Lord was washing him clean and filling him with His own forgiving love to flow out to these two men. As he lingered in Jesus' Presence, he received that comfort of all comforts, God's own forgiveness. Nothing in the entire world can substitute for God forgiving us. It is Divine!

When he returned to work, God had lifted a huge burden from him, namely separation from God. It was far easier than he had ever imagined to ask these men to forgive him even as he forgave them. His witness as to how the power of the Holy Spirit had changed him, so touched these men, that the Holy Spirit as the Spirit of Reconciliation, came down and reunited them as friends (Rom 13:8–10). When we have been wounded by others, we do not want to forgive, but the actual truth is we cannot forgive unless the Holy Spirit empowers us to love not with human love, but with Calvary Love.

Only in daily intentional prayer, can we learn to reach Jesus. By becoming more and more receptive to the voice and love of the Holy Spirit flooding us with the Reality of God's eternal love for us, will these changes come. As we experience time and again God's amazing generosity in forgiving us, we are enabled to forgive others.

So serious is this need for forgiving love, that at the end of the Lord's Prayer, Jesus repeats the imperative need to forgive our self and others. "If we do not forgive others, He will not forgive us" (Matt 6:14–15).

Are you outside the cycle of receiving and giving His love? Has some person or circumstance choked your receiving and giving God's love? If so, you are in a grave and serious situation. You cannot receive God's help apart from your crying out to Him in repentance and forgiveness to everyone.

Jesus, by His great sacrifice, has made available to all of us all the loving forgiveness we will ever need in this life. Will you let Him help you?

13

God's Power to Rescue

Lead us not into temptation but deliver us from evil.
Matthew 6:13

FOR MANY years our praying community has sought to lean heavily on the ministry of the Holy Spirit. Since He is the true Intercessor, and knows how to pray the will of God in all matters, we have sought to allow Him greater and ever greater access to our private and corporate praying (Rom 8:26–27).

It is exciting but often deeply painful to receive His wisdom and instruction in all aspects of the prayer life. Rev. J. Stuart Holden, M. A. has said, "Praying in the Holy Ghost is but co-operating with the will of God, and such prayer is always victorious. Be filled with the Spirit, who is the Spirit of grace and supplication."

Of all the Prayer Principles of the Sermon on the Mount, His ministry to us in our prayer chamber daily is of utmost importance. If we will allow Him to lovingly but compellingly confront, convict, correct, and cleanse our sins, faults, attitudes, and motives, we will find an ongoing restoration of our interior life, which releases us to a greater extent into Jesus' life.

The great saints have a term they use which is "despair of flesh." This phrase speaks of the anguish of perceiving our sinful fallen flesh and how necessary it is to correctly view it as a condition which only He can help. The Holy Spirit has been given to us as believers so we can come to know there is no way to "clean up flesh" or "improve it with self help." He wants us to see how truly wretched we are; how completely helpless and powerless we are in our own strength to cleanse and heal our self (Rom 7:22–25).

It is a work of the Holy Spirit to cause us to no longer lean on our self-sufficiency, self-effort, self-confidence, self-focus. Rather that we be brought to such weakness and despair so all we can do is cry out to the Holy Spirit to help us. There is no help in us, only in Him. As He humbles us, empowering us to "own up in repentance," this brings us the sprit of contrition and openness which allows Him to work (Isaiah 66:2).

He must bring us repeatedly to the end of our self that we might begin to "let go and let Him" help us. *This is not pleasurable; it is terribly painful but so life-giving!* However, ever so slowly, He is weaning us away from self that we might cling to Him (Deut 4:4). Therefore this then enables us to repent when we need to do so (1 John 1:9; Luke 3:9, 16–17). Our selfishness begins to grieve us profoundly when we begin action to take over. As proud and arrogant as we are, only He can bring us to that place of desperately yearning not to grieve Him.

Second Corinthians 12:9 says it perfectly that only as we are brought low in weakness can His life of power be revealed in us. Therefore this poignant phrase, "Lead us not into temptation but deliver us from evil" is saying, it seems to me, "Lord, You and You alone know all about me—my sins and failures, my inabilities and true weaknesses. Help me Jesus, Holy Spirit, to stay close to you, depending on You alone. Empower me, Holy Spirit to move towards a holy obedience to Your will and way. May I never wander away deliberately leaving You. Teach me all I need to remain true in You (John 15:7–8).

Are you remaining close to Jesus so that you avoid the enemy's territory? If you fail, are you penitent in an ever increasing despair of flesh? Will you surrender increasingly to the keeping power of the Indwelling Holy Spirit?

14

He Is Everything

For Thine is the Kingdom, the Power,
and the Glory forever. Amen.
Matthew 6:13

IT IS generally understood that this concluding phrase was added at a later time, but it is considered a most appropriate close to the prayer. The Lord Jesus Christ is the center of everything. He is the core, the foundation, the above and beyond. He is the center of our world, which He made (John 1:10). He is the center of the world that is to come (Revelation 7:9–12).

That we can, by the redemptive life of Jesus Christ, be made a friend of God, through Jesus' blood and the Holy Spirit within us is the miracle of all the ages (John 15:15).

Jesus begins this prayer by telling us that our Heavenly Father—supernatural being—lives in a Heavenly realm. His prayer ends with saying God the Father, God the Son, God the Holy Spirit, is the Kingdom, Power and Glory forever, and ever! We will see the actuality of our soon coming King as He reveals His Kingdom, Power and Glory here on this broken, wounded planet.

This Trinity is not interested in a solitary, isolated journey distanced from us, but the Godhead yearns for the loving companionship of each one of us relating to Him daily. He longs to manifest His Holy, Sacred Presence to us in ever new openness and directness (John 14:21–23).

The ever unfolding of His life in us and to us is life's greatest possible experience. I have found through every decade of my life, a larger, more satisfying, fulfilling relationship with Father, Son, and Holy Spirit. A river of love flows between us, a closeness that words can never fully express. He Himself becomes increasingly all in all. A communion of such sweetness and fire, give and take, yearning and completeness reveals to us that He is truly the treasure of all the ages. He is our redeemer in every situation; He is nearer than hands or feet. The transcendent, Eternal God lives within us and *will never leave us or forsake us* (Heb 13:5). I can ultimately lose everything and every one, but He will remain through all the reaches of eternity.

Jesus is the King of the Kingdom. He has all power given to Him in earth and Heaven (Matt 28:18); He is the brightness of God's glory and the express image of God's Person, upholding all things by the Word of His Power (Heb 1:3).

Everything we have ever longed for, everything we have been trying to find to fill our aching loneliness and pain, *Jesus is the answer*! He always has been, He always will be. There is no one like Jesus Christ, our Crucified and Risen Lord. He is revealed to us by the Holy Spirit in our human spirit (John 16:13–15).

Amen means, "So be it—so shall it be." God's ultimate plan of love and restoration in His children and this planet will triumph. All praise to Father, Son, and Holy Spirit.

Will you give Him an ever enlarging wedge of your time? All of the saints have taught that it takes time for us to get to God and it takes time for God to get to us. He yearns to have a close, warm communion with you. May each one of us truly pray from our deepest heart; the prayer of all prayers in these unsettling days.

15

He Meets Our Every Need

*Seek ye first the Kingdom of God and His righteousness,
and all these things shall be added to you.*
Matthew 6:33

THERE IS one last great Prayer Principle to share in
Matthew chapter 6. This principle is life changing in
its scope; it is in Matthew 6:19–34. To our awe and wonder,
it emerges as we come to our prayer closet faithfully each
day. So earth bound and flesh born are we that we have not
a clue what God desires for us in that prayer time. But the
unfolding of God's life in us through the many changes of
the passing days and years must truly be experienced to be
believed. As we close the door to the outside world we are
so unaware of the realm, into which we enter.

Simply put the principle is this. As we begin to breathe
the pure air and perfume of the King and His Kingdom
into our human nostrils it seeps down into our soul and
spirit ever so slowly. Here begins a journey of transformation in our thought life, all our emotions and desires, our
motives and intent, our realities, and our very being—the
deepest self. This is a painful confrontation with God and
self because we are full of self-will and self-love. However,
He always comes in such loving compassion for us that He
wins us over to Himself. If we will go with Him, He is allowed progressively more access to us and to the person He
wants us to be. He desires a totalitarian take over of control.

He wants to increase, but we must decrease (John 3:30). He wants us to know we can do nothing, but He can do all things (John 5:19–30). This is the essence of self-surrender. This is the heart of what spending time with God entails.

As this Heavenly renovation begins there is a springing up in us of more love for Father, Son, and Holy Spirit, through the inner ministry of the Holy Spirit (Rom 5:5). As this tiny trickle of love for Him begins we have no idea of the force of the mighty river of His love for us. It flows from this river which has already birthed our love for Him. But as we come daily His love for us will fan a flame of consuming love for Him. Out of this love exchange will come our deepening surrender to Him as He is allowed to cleanse us on every level of our being. This is the most thrilling journey in the world. Experiencing Him in this way is so exciting, so loving and so kind, yet correcting us and empowering us to change.

These life renewing interactions will give Him more and more authority over us and in us. The Spirit of faith quickens more trust in Him because we know Him better (2 Cor 4:13) and love Him as never before.

Amazing changes begin as we let go of worries over job, shelter, food, family, the future, and ourselves. He has promised to take care of us and He will if we walk in obedience to His word and voice (1 Pet 5:7). We say again there are many wrestlings with God over the years. There are many difficult and hard times in allowing Him to confront us in great love (Gen 32:24–31). But, oh how worthwhile to be more and more open to His inner workings in our soul and spirit!

We begin to understand how terrible sin is and we do not want to offend Him. We do not want to wound Him by any deliberate sin, and yet we know many resistances to Him remain. When we do wrong and sin against His love, we are deeply repentant, and find we must have His forgiveness—willing to make any restitution necessary. When we are serious about our walk with God our Father, the Holy Spirit our Helper, and Jesus our Redeemer, they are so inviting that we love each member of the Trinity in an ever increasing way (John 14:16–17).

This continually deepening relationship is founded on daily coming to Him, of being connected to Him, and learning to stay connected all through the day. The presence of Jesus is so comforting in our life that it becomes easier to allow Him to be King of our little kingdom here on earth (John 17:9 17). Daily prayer is the place of learning to love Him more and more and to allow Him to flow through us to everyone that we meet.

He is allowed ever increasing power over all our circumstances. In our praying community we continue to see profound changes in one another. We have a long journey yet to make, but we know Him in a different way today than when we started. He is teaching all of us how to let Him be Lord in all our needs and problems.

Will you enter into this prayer pilgrimage and find Him able to take care of everything if we will let Him have His way? To miss this transforming adventure is to miss everything. To truly allow Him to be more and more first in our time, our relationships, is to walk in His righteousness allowing Him to be "all in all."

In closing I pray you will experience this ever growing shift in focus and emphasis from our being in control of our lives to allowing Him to be everything to us. He wants to be the King of our Kingdom and cleanse us from all unrighteousness. Obadiah 1:17 tells us to "possess our possessions" and it is a growing joy to see what we truly possess because of this relationship with Him.

If we are cultivating our life with God, every decade will bring profound changes in our concept of God the Father, God the Son, and God the Holy Spirit.

16

Are Jesus' Attitudes Active in Us?

And seeing the multitudes, he went up into a mountain:
and when he was set, his disciples came unto him:
and he opened his mouth, and taught them . . .
Matthew 5:1–2

NOWHERE IN the Bible do we see the attitudes of Jesus Christ spoken in any more stark contrast to our society and culture, than in these bold proclamations in the Sermon on the Mount. From the extremes of desperate, bitter need to the fulfillment of that need through the power of God Himself, we see the colossal extremity of total opposites to the fullest measure. These attitudes we should be or the *Be*atitudes are actually the direct result of time spent with God in the prayer life.

1. "Blessed are the poor in spirit: for theirs is the kingdom of heaven" (Matt 5:3).

Foundational to all spiritual growth and fulfillment of need is the solitude and quiet of the prayer closet which allows for the increasing awareness of the contrast between Father, Son and Holy Spirit and myself. As frightening as it is to see and know our fallenness, it is necessary for each one of us to know the dark pit of our inability to help ourselves in any way (1 Cor 3:1–6).

God gives us a great gift when He helps us to see how broken, powerless, and helpless we are in our own resources and strengths. The most appalling reality is the downward pull of our sinful fallen nature (Rom 3:10–18)!

When we first begin facing our many deficiencies, weaknesses, and insecurities it is shocking and frightening, but if you will allow Him to help you, He will aid you in every way possible. The Holy Work of the Indwelling Holy Spirit, Jesus and Father is a *mammoth work*, which only They can do (John 14:21, 23). To gently, but truly, pull back the barriers we have built up, the pretenses and facades we have erected, the shocking dishonesty and sinfulness from which only our Holy and Righteous Ancient of days, the Lord God Almighty is able to redeem us (Acts 9:1–16).

In a way that is most wondrous, He begins to show us that the need itself contains the Divine answer. Only as He brings us low in humility do we begin to see the truth of our total inability to save ourselves. He gives grace and mercy to empower us to allow Him to help us. Not only does He work in our inner life, but He gets in the middle of our outer circumstances by allowing failure, dissatisfaction, humiliation and bitter disappointment. Our dear Teacher, the Holy Spirit, begins to pull back all the grief-stained layers of self-love, and self-will which usually have helped to create our many problems (Jer 2:17–19). To cover our limitations of all kinds, we have sought to hide our envy, jealousy, loneliness, anger, lovelessness, unworthiness by levels of dishonesty that only He can ferret out and heal (1 John 1:9).

I do not know of any more tender or life-giving episodes with God, then when our wonderful Holy Spirit begins the "uncovering" of our lies to ourselves. He loves us so totally there is no condemnation of any kind, only a massive "soul and spirit redeeming love" as He gently shows us our chronic sins and needs that so terribly cut us off from Him.

It is Jesus' own unconditional grace and love for us that can empower us to see our need, and help us take personal ownership over our sins against our self and others (John 4:4–30).

He and He alone bring us to the place of being able finally, to face our self, and *face Him*.

He alone brings heart and soul healing and peace. He actually does it all Himself—bringing us low where we see the truth of ourselves—giving us courage to turn to Him, and being able, by His grace, to receive His mercy and healing.

How then do we come to a place of facing our self? How do we receive the courage to see the pure truth of total helplessness? How do we endure His Holy Presence as He lovingly speaks eternal Truth to us? We have found in our praying community we must be willing in our times alone with Him to release all our control and self-will the best we can—to cry out for His will, no matter what it takes.

The Beatitudes reveal to us many truths of what is our part and what is God's part in our seasons of prayer. We begin to understand this ever so slowly, that in essence He has to do it all to bring us to a lowly posture where He will empower us to be able to receive His ministry to us.

Only God Almighty could break through all the barriers of our selfhood which we have erected over the years. Not any easy task, as we live in a veritable fortress, which we feel necessary to survive.

When we begin to come we usually are not poor in spirit, but rather our defenses are strong and virtuous. As we come day after day, we find so much of our help from God comes as we allow Him *time* to help us face ourselves and our need. We have so many misconceptions of Him and our self, but the beginning point each day is inviting Him to reveal whatever He wants me to see, that I might know on all levels of my being my complete and total dependency on Him.

He slowly and lovingly brings His empowerment to me to face whatever pain and anguish that is in me. With the Holy Spirit quickening me with supernatural strength, I begin to learn by His compassion, I can be aware of my inner poverty and survive to tell the story! The King of the Kingdom offers Himself!

> 2. "Blessed are they that mourn for they shall be com-
> forted" (Matt 5:4).

To mourn is to suffer such unspeakable, great sadness that no human can relieve. Only our precious Heavenly Father, the God of all comfort, can touch the very core of unbearable pain (2 Cor 1:3–10). The ministry of the Indwelling Holy Spirit can so draw us to Jesus and Jesus to Father that the very Presence of the Godhead will bring peace, comfort, and hope. One of the unchangeable lessons of the Sermon on the Mount is that to be in bitter need involves all our energies. It is a totalitarian experience. As the Holy Spirit gently draws us to come to Jesus and Father, our energies begin to be drawn to another source, that of God Himself. He can be found as the answer to all our need, when we seek Him with all our hearts (Jer 29:13). Only He can gather and redirect our energies to Him, where alone we find solace.

I feel concern over so little time being spent alone in Jesus Presence, by so many Christians. Often people are there so briefly He does not have the opportunity to manifest Himself (John 14:21). He has much to teach us about receiving His ministry to us. We spend so much time in and with the world there is little time to spend with Him (Dan 9:3–19; Matt 6:33).

In our praying community we have seen God's comfort abound in so many of life's tragedies of loss and grief. He has taught us over the years to lay aside whatever is claiming our attention and time so we can come closer to Him, but more importantly allow Him to come closer to us (Jas 4:8).

3. "Blessed are the meek for they shall inherit the earth" (Matt 5:5).

Only our beloved Father, Son, and Holy Spirit, can by one episode after another, in the prayer closet, bring us to a place where we flee from self-aggression, self-assertiveness, and all inner and outer forms of bossy, cocky, self-focused conduct. Our Lord's humility and submissive conduct as they took Him from the garden, and all through the trial, culminating on the Cross in such selfless obedience to God, was such that it literally ripped Heaven and Earth apart.

As we meditate on this, we cry out in despair to be cleansed of our center stage mentality. We yearn to be more like Him, whatever it takes (John 18–19)! Only in an unconditional surrender daily at the feet of Jesus, allowing Him to take over more and more in a moment to moment yieldedness, can we be empowered to be emptied out of self that He might increase, and we decrease (John 3:30).

4. "Blessed are they which do hunger and thirst after righteousness for they shall be filled" (Matt 5:6).

As Jesus, Holy Spirit, and Father come to us over and over again in Heavenly, Divine love restoring, cleansing, drawing us to a whole new reality, we find such yearning growing in our heart. "Lord, I want to be more and more yours, I want to be like you, hopeless as that seems! You are life itself—I do not want to live the way I have been living anymore—teach me how to let you be Lord and Master. Teach me how to live with You." Only time with Him creates a deepening hunger for more of Him. When I was a serious pianist practicing many, many hours a day, I always wanted to practice more, but when I practiced little, I wanted to do little. In other words, little time with Jesus, little desire to be with Jesus.

> 5. "Blessed are the merciful: for they shall obtain mercy" (Matt 5:7).

As our ever merciful and gracious Lord continues to show us His unending grace and mercy in our daily encounters with Him in the prayer closet, He begins to alter our attitudes so they are full of the mercy and grace He is giving us. It is profoundly touching and transforming to experience His mercy, time after time, in our prayer processing in the secret place of prayer. We are moved to respond in a more merciful attitude only as we are touched by His unchanging love for us. To receive Jesus' forgiveness, the wisdom of the Holy Spirit, the love of God for us individually, is to be changed more into His image. Truly and absolutely, the greatest experience of this life is a growing, interacting relationship with Father, Son and Holy Spirit (John 1:14).

> 6. "Blessed are the pure in heart: for they shall see God" (Matt 5:8).

When you have put your roots down in a praying community for over twenty-five years you begin to see the ongoing transformation of people who started so burdened with over involvement of life's activities, living pretty much as they wanted to live the Christian life, over scheduled, overwhelmed, saturated with many affections and idols of our culture. It is a glorious journey to see Father, Son, and Holy Spirit pruning, convicting, cleansing, stripping away all excess baggage until He begins to emerge in each one of us as Lord over more and more of our entire beings. A revolution truly begins as we gather weekly for prayer on a solid foundation of increasing daily time with God.

Our purposes, goals, desires begin to flow into one channel, a single, passionate desire to stay in the Presence of

Father, Son, and Holy Spirit in obedient, loving surrender. To love Him with all our heart, soul, mind, and strength is our goal. We have a long journey to make, but we are not where we were and not yet what we shall become, but how glorious to walk with Him every inch of the way!

> 7. "Blessed are the peace makers: for they shall be called the children of God" (Matt 5:9).

There are throngs of people today who have no inner peace because true peace is only in our Blessed Lord Jesus Christ. We cannot give out His peace, unless He rules and reigns in our hearts. We cannot give what we do not have. Only in an ever growing dependency on Him, giving Him time to manifest His Presence, to settle us down within by revealing our present needs and issues. In our ready obedience of all He is speaking, being willing to allow Him to be Lord over all of our inner and outer life. He is ever bringing His Eternal, Divine Peace to us daily so we can become instruments of His peace. His living Presence in us will flow out of us in compassion and peace to others, but it is only as we stay under His wing (Ps 91:1).

There is no human, earthly way to have the Peace of Heaven, real and undisturbed in us without the daily soaking of ourselves in the Divine Peace of our Eternal Father, Son, and Holy Spirit.

The last two Beatitudes, Matthew 5:10–11 need our attention in a world in which there is much suffering and persecution.

> 8. "Blessed are they which are persecuted for righteousness sake: for theirs is the Kingdom of Heaven" (Matt 5:10).

> 9. "Blessed are ye, when men shall revile you and persecute you, and shall say all manner of evils against you falsely, for my sake" (Matt 5:11).

As you well know, there is much reviling and persecution going on in our world. I believe Jesus is saying firstly, that this is not our home. Secondly, that there is an enormous price on our heads as Christians. Think of Jesus and the deathly price He paid to crush the enemy's power and render him helpless. Thirdly, we will enter the fellowship of His sufferings (Phil 3:10) each one of us, in whatsoever means He sees fit. Matthew 5:12 says for us to ". . . rejoice and be exceedingly glad: for great is your reward in Heaven: for so persecuted they the prophets which were before you."

Suffering, affliction, and chastisement all play a vital part in our unfolding life with God.

Second Corinthians 4:5–11 says, "we are troubled on every side, yet not distressed; we are perplexed, but not in despair; persecuted, but not forsaken; cast down, but not destroyed always bearing about in the body the dying of the Lord Jesus that the life also of Jesus might be made manifest in our body. For we which live are always delivered unto death for Jesus sake, that the life of Jesus also might be made manifest in our mortal flesh."

There is no way in the flesh we can ever measure up to the standard of the Beatitudes, never in a million years. It must be *Jesus Himself* living in us and our constant submission to His Lordship, that through the Holy Spirit's ministry, He lives His life in and through us, according to Father's great redemption plan.

How the world needs Christians who are meeting with Jesus daily, and allowing Him permission to get down into the midst of our attitudes and reactions so that He is allowed to live more fully His life in and through our life. Are you meeting with Him daily, and allowing the Holy Spirit to point the way to Jesus' Lordship in all that you do and say?

17

He Can Turn
Our Darkness to Light

But the comforter, which is the Holy Ghost,
whom the Father will send in My name, He shall
teach you all things, and bring all things to your
remembrance, whatsoever I have said unto you.
John 14:26

IF YOU are increasingly asking the Holy Spirit to reveal Himself to you in this Prayer Experiment, hopefully you are finding that it is an awesome and powerful experience. With anticipation you are allowing Him to shed His light and love on your inner thought life. His life of love will make your motives and intentions increasingly more visible to you. As we open ourselves to Him, He will cast His loving light on our interior thought life.

The passage for study in this chapter is Matthew 5:13–20. His victorious and risen life in us is to be as salt and light in the world. Though we cannot see Him, we experience Him working within in ways that cannot be denied. In experiences that are challenging and we do not know what to do, as we wait on Him, He will give us light or understanding as to what to do.

The Holy Spirit acting as salt within us penetrates deep within our soul and spirit (Gal 4:19). He cleanses us (Ps 51:6–7). He preserves His life in us (Col 1:27). He enhances and seasons all of our life in Him (John 15:7). He makes attractive and approachable His life in us (1 John 2:3–6).

The Holy Spirit acting as light within us causes us to see light (Ps 36:9). He sows light like seed for the righteous (Ps 97:11). He causes light to arise in the darkness for the upright (Ps 112:4).

His life in us is mysterious, yet very concrete. This enables us, through Him, to fulfill right doing in the inner life. This gives His anointing power in the outer life. Only as the inner life is brought into loving obedience to the nature of Jesus can the outer life be righteous. The inner and outer being in harmony through the Holy Spirit, result in a righteousness that exceeds the Scribes and Pharisees because their power lies only in the outer act while the heart is cold and outside Jesus (Matt 15:7–9).

Jesus is saying in the Sermon on the Mount that He looks to the heart (Matt 6:21) and its condition. Our prayers are answered according to our inner condition of faith and love. He looks to the inner, not the pretended or assumed outer condition of the heart or spirit. In verses 17–20 of Matthew chapter 5 He says His imperatives for answering prayer will never be changed or altered in any way. Heaven and earth will pass away, but His laws and commandments will never be changed for anyone. The great power of the Holy Spirit is that He teaches us, as we pray, how to align ourselves with the way He functions. We learn to submit to His rules and conditions. We want to be in honest inner harmony with Him so that the outer life might be publicly righteous.

There are definite signs that the Holy Spirit is at work in us as salt and light. The great souls throughout all ages have taught that there are definite results from His activity within us. I want to list some of those major signs of His being salt and light:

- All the time and everywhere we are dealing with God alone. Not individuals, not groups, not circumstances, only God (Jer 10:10–12)! There are no second causes. In the inner life of our attitudes and thoughts, we must submit to Him as being the One with whom we have to deal and surrender to His will and way. In that releasing of ourselves to Him, He bring us to a deeper need for more of Him and His love, we learn to trust Him more and we die to a deeper level of our selfishness and control. We deal then in all situations only with Him (Luke 23:39–46)!

- When we open our attitudes and thoughts to the Holy Spirit and His word, two inevitable results occur:

    * Great darkness begins to rise up in us, confusion, alienation, desolation, loneliness, and fear.
    * There are many areas that are hidden from our awareness and He will allow these painful experiences to rise up in us that He may help us to deal with them.

William Connolly, a current Catholic priest, is writing on various aspects of prayer. He says it so well, and I quote,

- Fears—basic fear of God begins to emerge, we are afraid we will lose who we are, we fear God will abandon us and get fed up with us, there is a fear of loneliness in us in deep places that God has not touched yet, there are barricaded places we dance around, desolations we know nothing about.

- Angers—over our past there is righteous anger and unrighteous anger toward God and others, anger over pain others have given us, not meeting our expectations, anger toward ourself.

- Guilt—most awful guilt is that we cannot live up to our ideas of ourselves, and we hate ourselves for it, guilt over doing wrong, hurting others, and hatred we have of those who hurt us.[1]

The saints for centuries have taught that any and all darkness rising in us in prayer is a form of resistance to God. That darkness can become so awful we abandon all forms of prayer and run from God, who is allowing the darkness to surface so that He might help us (Ps 51:6–7). We know that out of the fear of facing our inner darkness we run from God and refuse the help that only He can offer. The busy lives we enforce on ourselves keep the fears, angers and guilt from bringing us to the terrible reality of our helplessness and inadequacy. Father Connolly believes our perfectionism insulates us from discovering our frightening condition.

What are we to do, as the rising darkness comes forth? *Cry out to the Holy Spirit and acknowledge your helplessness.* St. Teresa of Avila would say, "Slide down into the grave of nothingness." Hang on to Jesus for dear life, He is your teacher (John 14:6) and He will guide you; ask for His wisdom to know the truth about any and all circumstances. Bless His name for surfacing the darkness from deep within you, as you pray.

If we keep suppressing the darkness because we would rather avoid the pain, the Holy Spirit cannot deal with us as He dealt with Paul and thousands of other Christians down through the ages. *The Holy Spirit is the Helper.* Are you allowing Him to help you?

The great inner struggle with darkness and pain begins to surface so that God, the Holy Spirit might help us. The fear of losing control can be great, but learning that there is nothing we can do to save ourselves is the reality we must

1. Conley, "Experiences of Darkness in Directed Retreats," 108–14.

face. This allows God in His mercy to shower on us His grace and mercy.

Our deepest failure is often not allowing Him time to deal with us. It takes time in His Presence to give Him the opportunity to reveal His will and for us to yearn to please Him (Phil 2:13).

He wants to teach us how to enter into dialogue with Him. How to listen, how to talk together, how to relate to Him, is how you get in touch with what you are feeling. This is a major issue. To speak aloud to Him or to write in your journal is helpful. How to prayerfully process with Him, your dearest and truest Friend, is the transforming quality of a prayer life.

He will often move you into peace even though all components of your feelings are not yet dealt with. Let Him deal with you as He will, according to His agenda and not yours. He knows the timing and progression that we uniquely need in order to deal with every aspect of our emotional life. Prayer is to allow the deepest levels of our feelings and pain to bring us to Jesus in an ever deepening surrender and trust even as we see our helplessness and failures.

I want to close by quoting from Mary Welch, who was a great woman of prayer from the early part of this century. The following three powerful statements come from her interaction with the Holy Spirit.

1. "Deep cleansing in prayer is intended to bring us to the point in prayer where we pray that we might receive the things *God needs to give us*, to fulfill His purposes for us." We are called according to His purposes, not our purposes (Rom 8:28).

2. In deepening personal prayer we throw away all alibis, self-pity, fear of peoples' opinions, and slavery to their understanding or misunderstanding,

and finally my rights and cravings to be right about everything.

3. We do not need to depend on the ones we give to, to be the ones who give to us, so love all unconditionally! He is released to meet our needs ". . . according to His riches in glory" (Phil 4:19).[2]

Therefore the Holy Spirit desires us to accept on an ever deepening level the reality of our weaknesses and helplessness, that we might give Him access to us to let His strength come forth. Will you welcome this work of the Holy Spirit?

Many times when our inner darkness arises, it is so overwhelming we may need to seek professional help. If you need that kind of help to come along side of you, please seek it out. To do that does not make you a bad person or a poor Christian.

---

2. These three statements are a summary of what Mary Welch describes in her booklet, *What Wilt Thou?: Three Steps to Creative Praying*.

18

The Holy Spirit Brings
Victory over Darkness

Let your light so shine before men, that
they may see your good works, and glorify
your Father which is in Heaven.
Matthew 5:16

WILLIAM CARY, the great missionary to India, once
said, "Going to India is like going into a deep, dark
well. I will descend if Jesus holds the rope."

Going deeper in prayer is much like going down into
a deep dark well, but Jesus holds the rope, praise His name.
Previously we talked about the darkness and emotional pain
that begins to emerge when we intentionally get into serious
prayer. As the darkness surfaces, we can learn to cling to
Jesus and allow Him time to cleanse and heal us. Actually,
our whole lifetime with Jesus is learning to allow Him more
and more opportunities to help us through cleansing, as we
wait on Him.

Morton T. Kelsey says, "The truest sign of maturity
is a willingness to endure immediate pain in order to find
an ultimate good. Neurosis is an unwillingness to look at
inner pain and allow God to work." Kelsey is a prominent
charismatic Episcopal priest who has written extensively on
the spiritual life.

As we allow Jesus time to minister to us, and deal with us on all the levels of our being, we find a deeper self-knowledge and hence a more willing spirit of clinging to Him. We need Him because we see our desperate need more clearly (1 John 1:5–10; Isa 51:3–4).

In this chapter we want to look at the tremendous gathering of external darkness that is in our sinful, fallen world. Only the blessed Holy Spirit can make sense of all this, so we can have a sense of peace in Him (Eph 2:14). Only He can sustain us in the midst of grave outer confusion and give us spiritual understanding.

There is a growing sadness, an enveloping sadness within us as we see the tragic circumstances of our world. We feel a deepening grief, impending disaster, and growing confusion in the world system. We know God is allowing all of it, that we might humble ourselves before Him and repent, both personally and nationally. The pain and suffering in the world is increasing. There is hardly one family today that does not have at least one serious problem confronting them. To come through victoriously it will only be by the power of the Holy Spirit.

Our humanity is under enormous pressure, Jesus' second coming is near, I believe. Our redemption draweth nigh! We have increasing joy and desire to see Jesus and go home, but our hearts burn within us for our families, friends, church, nation, and world (Jer 9).

This passionate concern for others, mingled with grief over the pain that is needed to bring people to their knees, is greatly taxing on our body (stress), mind (anxiety) and spirit (grief). Intercessors allow the grief and sadness, the yearning for others to find God to bring them to the throne of grace. Then the Holy Spirit can weep and lament through us, praying the prayers of God for the people of the world.

Jesus is seeking to train us for battle, by our drawing closer to Him, and hiding in His Presence (Ps 27:5–6). Only in what the saints have called "bridal love" or "first love" for Jesus can we survive these days. In a deepening union with His will and purpose He becomes more real to us than any other person, and there is a love flowing between us that keeps us obedient and humble.

We need to remember that He is our only protection, and only in Him, the cleft of the rock, are we safe (Song 2:14). Our actual experience in Jesus and with Jesus will be all that we finally need. All else will crumble and fail, but He wants to protect us in all realms—in the *physical* realm, with proper rest, food, exercise; the *spiritual* realm with much time with Jesus, that we might decrease and He increase; in the *emotional* realm, He wants to unlock our bolted doors one after another that we might be healed from emotional scars and wounds.

The pressure and stress is so monumental that you and I will often feel that we want to escape from their grasp (Ps 55:1–8). The Psalmist gives perfect expression to what you and I often will feel. We must allow the Holy Spirit full sway in showing us when we are indeed weary and needing rest, when indeed we need to "run away" from all the emotional and mental stress. He desires a deep balance in us, as we are anchored in Him, body, soul, and spirit (1 Thess 5:23). The Scriptures teach that there is a time needed for retreat and meditation and it is called Biblical Sabbath Rest. It is a time set apart for rest, relaxation, and privacy that is so necessary. It is time that we might seek Him, rest in Him, and wait on Him so He can minister to us (Heb 4:9–11; Ezek 44:15–17).

In the prayer life we allow the Holy Spirit to reveal to us what we have brought on ourselves; what God is saying; what the enemy is doing; and what the sins of others against us have done to us, which causes us to sin against them! In the growing relationship with the Holy Spirit we see more clearly what is actually happening in all of our life's circumstances. He will give wisdom and understanding, insight and discernment as we wait on Him (Matt 11:28–30).

I have found these examples of Paul's intensive daily challenges, that he took into the inner sanctuary of his prayer closet, to be revealing and instructive. He lived out of utter powerlessness in and of himself, but with a humble dependency on God alone.

He knew his own helplessness and emptiness, but he knew even more about the supernatural life of God living within him. The deeper his insufficiency, the more God could flow through him.

May you and I learn from Paul's prayer life that this level of victory comes from the indwelling Godhead alone as we daily process every need with Him. (Unfortunately the author does not know the source of the following excellent list.)

> **Acts 20:17–27** Living in God so deeply he was not disturbed by the future.
>
> **Acts 21:10–15** Nothing could dislodge his loyalty to God's character.
>
> **1 Corinthians 2:1–4** In weakness, fear, trembling he lived in God's strength.
>
> **1 Corinthians 16:9** Many adversaries did not faze him.
>
> **2 Corinthians 1:8–11** Despaired of life itself.
>
> **2 Corinthians 4:7–11** Death to self that Jesus might reveal His life in Paul.
>
> **2 Corinthians 6:1–10** Victory over all pain and affliction.
>
> **2 Corinthians 11:22–30** So detached from himself he took delight in helplessness.
>
> **2 Corinthians 12:7–11** As Paul kept close to God moment by moment he drew on God's healing power.

The only way to cross the bridge from our broken insufficiency is the Holy Spirit infusing us with the life of Jesus Christ. This is the essence of daily prayer! We can only learn this as we engage in relating to the Holy Spirit, Jesus, and Father. *This takes much time and patience!*

Will you turn to the Holy Spirit in your prayer time allowing Him to help you rather than you trying to help yourself? Ask the Holy Spirit to take over in interior prayer, as each troubled event comes to you, that He might pray God's will in each instance. Also ask Him, to continue to teach you how to abide in Him, no matter what comes, and to trust Him in the midst of a growing, exterior darkness (Gal 2:20). John 1:5 states, "The Light Shines in the darkness and the darkness has never overpowered it" *and it never will.*

19

How Do We Become More Yielded to God?

Behold thou desirest truth in the inward parts:
and in the hidden part thou shall make me to know
wisdom. Purge me with hyssop, and I shall be clean:
wash me, and I shall be whiter than snow.

Psalm 51:6–7

EARLIER I spoke briefly about my Mother's prayer life, but I want to expand on the unfolding of her time with God. It was a great privilege to witness the various ongoing stages and dimensions of her life with God.

In the years of child-rearing she would pour out her feelings, opinions, desires, concerns to her Heavenly Father when she first came to her prayer closet. This was usually after we three children were in school for the day. She was very honest and real, telling God exactly what she felt she needed Him to do in a particular circumstance. She was very serious about obeying the conditions of the promise she had taken into life's laboratory. We know that many of the nine thousand promises in the Bible have no conditions to be met on our part, but many prayer promises do have attitudes that must be activated in us by the Holy Spirit.

Then in the early afternoon she took a short nap. Awakening from her rest she would ask the Holy Spirit to respond to what she had asked in the morning. Relaxed, open, responsive she waited on God to reply in any way He felt necessary in response to her morning requests. Oftentimes He would confirm and yet lovingly correct her at the same time (John 10:4–5, 27).

As the years went by she became able, through the Holy Spirit and much practice, to tune into the compassionate loving voice of God (Ps 62:8). She always sought to give Him equal time to speak as she had taken time to share. To fail to give Him time to speak to her meant that she was being too busy. I remember one classic example of this. As I came home from high school one lovely autumn day, I found mother in the kitchen getting our supper ready for the oven.

"Mamma, what happened between you and God today?" I asked knowing that she had taken for her promise that day Philippians 4:6–7 "be careful for nothing; but in everything by prayer and supplication with thanksgiving let your requests be made known unto God. And the peace of God which passes all understanding, shall keep your hearts and minds through Christ Jesus." She was very serious about obeying the condition of not allowing any worry or anxiety to spread itself out over the situation for which she was praying at time.

She turned from her cooking with her eyes dancing. "The dear Holy Spirit said my worrying and fretting was hindering Him because I had no faith to believe Him to bring His answer. You cannot worry and trust God at the same time. You do not really believe I will do what is best."

It was so authoritative, I stopped short in the doorway. I felt the "holy hush" of God's Presence flowing out of my mother. "What did you say, Momma?" She flashed back a loving smile and said, "Margaret, there is no one like Jesus in the entire world! As He spoke to me I saw in a flash exactly what I was doing. The phrase *untroubled trust* rose up in my heart. He wants a rich, deep confidence in His character that knows no doubt and unbelief." That interaction of God and my mother has remained with me over the years and has profoundly affected my prayer life even today.

I saw over the years the life changing influences of God in my mother's life. These experiences have created in me a longing for the Holy Spirit to empower me to trust Jesus as the Holy Spirit does that I will learn to walk in "untroubled trust" or die in the attempt (2 Cor 4:13)!

I will never forget the Presence of the Holy Spirit revealing Jesus to my mother, in a new and transforming way, that crisp autumn day (John 16:13–15). There were many fresh and new changes in her as she continued to spend time with God day by day. She became a woman who not only talked "to" God, but they talked "with" one another.

The Prayer Experiment is learning to be a friend of God. It is dialogue between two people, whose relationship goes far out beyond a particular request.

There is so much cleansing He needs to do in us (John 6:53–58)! The James 4:3 passage says we can ask for the wrong thing. "Ye ask and receive not, because ye ask amiss, that ye may consume it on your lusts." Our possessiveness in wanting our own way, our attitudes of pride, vanity, and power indicate that we are not in touch with these areas when we pray. How we need time in waiting on Him so He can speak to us and cleanse us of areas so buried that we are oblivious of them.

Are you allowing time for Jesus to respond to your praying? He bends over you in eternal compassion to help you. If we are blocking Him in any way, we short circuit His answers. As He makes known to us our barriers in times of prayer we can give them to Him and allow Him to bring us victory at the former place of defeat.

What a thrilling experience to understand Him and our self better as the Holy Spirit tells us the truth about our self and our wonderful Lord. He embraces us as He lovingly corrects us.

20

Give God Time
to Respond to You

Be still and know that I am God.
Psalm 46:10

How then, in practical ways, do we allow God to respond to our asking, seeking, knocking (Luke 11:1–13)? My mother could interpret large truths in a simple succinct way. She would say, "People want to know three things about prayer. Does it work? How does it work? Will it work for me?"

On the foundation of these three poignant questions, I want to share some of the simple tenants of waiting on God. There is much that could be said as the topic is extensive, but how do we begin in a humble, down to earth, yet close to Heaven way? For those who are interested, this is dealt with in detail in my book, *Realizing The Presence of the Spirit*.

In the deepest sense, it is a matter of "settling down" in God's Presence, a learning to calm down and relax with Him so the Holy Spirit can begin to teach us how to relate to Father, Son, and Holy Spirit. A daily place of quietness and solitude, private and shut away, the prayer closet, which is spoken of in Matthew 6:6, with no interruptions, a place to let go of busyness and focus on Him, not ourselves. There are four things that should be remembered.

First, when you sit down, begin by asking the Holy Spirit to reveal Jesus to you (John 16:13–15). Only the Holy Spirit can show us Jesus, as He pulls back the veil of our human spirit so we can see Him in fresh, revitalizing, personal ways. If we fail to ask for the Holy Spirit's help, we plunge into our trying to focus on Him out of our need of control which releases our self-will, self-reliance, and self-sufficiency. These "self" qualities are the major hindrances to realizing His Presence.

Our whole life is contaminated with the "taking over" maneuvers of the self-life. To wait on Him is an opportunity to practice laying down all self management, all manipulation of trying to force God to act, all the strength of our will to have our own way.

Needless to say, we need the Spirit of God, the Spirit of Jesus, in and through the Holy Spirit living within the Christian to help us. The Holy Spirit is the Helper (John 15:16–18, 26)! Are you able through Him to receive His help?

It is far better to sit and do nothing for 20–30 minutes than to take control of the situation. To wait quietly is a means of giving God a more open entrance into your heart. If we have asked the Holy Spirit to teach and lead us to Jesus, we need to learn how to follow His leadings.

There is an undoing of our twisted theology that we are in charge of the time with God which is presumptuous and false (Ps 19:13–14). The blessed Holy Spirit is in charge of my prayer life. He is the intercessor (Rom 8:26) and He wants to unfold His ministry of helpfulness to us as we give the reins to Him. It is in daily waiting on God we learn what absolute, unconditional surrender really means.

My mother would often say, "Every morning I go to God's school. I sit down in my little desk and look up at my Teacher and He opens up the ministry of prayer and waiting to me."

Secondly, relax the best you can, ask the Holy Spirit to empower you to let go of all need to fix things; all striving and straining to do it yourself; all need to be successful at being with God. All the saints of history say it takes much time to learn to be quiet, responsive and focused on Jesus because we are so full of our self. We cannot in the flesh bring about God's Presence. His Presence, Himself, is the greatest of gift of all! The precious Holy Spirit always points to Jesus and Jesus to the Father.

If you are a high achiever, letting go of doing it yourself will be difficult because all of your issues of self go deep and keep each one of us from yieldedness and submission to Him. But as you persist, He will work inside of you, and out of His sheer mercy and grace, your inner life to Him will be unlocked.

Thirdly, if after a time of humbly waiting on the Holy Spirit to guide you, and guidance does not seems to come, quietly do what you feel most drawn to do in responding to God. You may feel encouraged to read in your Bible, or to pray for yourself or others. Perhaps you are drawn to read from a classic book on prayer, or simply sitting and just loving Father, Son, and Holy Spirit. How powerful this is to adore Him, worship Him, to thank Him for all He is, and how He has helped you over and over again. Use this time to give your whole being to Him. Afresh and anew, great cleansing comes to us as we love Him with all our heart, soul, and being.

Lastly, actually, to linger in Jesus' Presence and allow as full an expression of love to Him as you can, and then allow Him to love you back is the closeness for which we are so hungry. This will continually open up to you the priceless gift of Himself—Father, Son, and Holy Spirit. As you come into His Presence over the months and years, He will be more and more real to you.

The potent thrust of the Sermon on the Mount is that He seeks all of our inner and outer life to be met and conquered by Him. Living from the inside out giving Him free rein. Will you and I allow Him to be all in all?

21

Anger Turned to Love

But I say unto you, love your enemies, bless them that
curse you, do good to them that hate you, and pray for
them which despitefully use you, and persecute you.
Matthew 5:44

AT THE outset of this chapter I want to briefly review
what has been said about our Prayer Experiment. We
are taking very seriously the Sermon on the Mount, and
the attitudes that bring blessing and peace (Matt 5:1–12).
These are actually qualities of Divine Love that are necessary
ingredients in God's will for the releasing of His answers to
our prayers.

In Matthew 7:1–14 we have entered into the morti-
fication of no judgment and no criticism. God will honor,
beyond our furthermost imagination, any of His children
seeking to live in love rather than judgment. The lack of
judgment releases prayers being answered beyond all
expression.

The last three chapters have dealt with allowing the
Holy Spirit to search out our darkness of sin and selfishness (Matt 7:1–14). Here we will look at Matthew 5:21–26.
Jesus lists four negative and dangerous attitudes or emotions, which must be searched out and handled in our daily
life. These emotions hinder our prayer life and must be
resolved.

The first emotion is *anger* (Matt 5:21–26). The second highly inflammable emotion is *lust* (Matt 5:27–32). The third dangerous emotion is a *pride and arrogance* to God's laws and will (Matt 5:33–37). The fourth emotion is retaliation, or getting even with others (Matt 5:38–42).

Jesus mentions four different levels of anger in this passage, and each level will bring consequences that are inevitable. This forceful emotion must be handled by the Holy Spirit almost on a daily basis in our prayer life.

1. Angry with brother or sister—to malign, or speak evil of, be malicious and very harmful where our brother/sister is concerned—we shall be guilty before the court.

2. Whoever says, "Raca," shall appear before the supreme or Sanhedrin council. It is an attitude or anger that says, "You are beyond loving, you are not worth loving." It is very disparaging of another person.

3. Whoever says, "You fool," shall be guilty enough to go to "the fiery hell," because it is a total demeaning, as if the person did not exist.

4. To allow anger to produce murder is liable to the courts. A most tragic consequence to an emotion.

What is Jesus saying in this passage? I believe He is wanting us to know that though killing is a great sin, anger is also a sin. A sin because we can abandon God's love and are pushed out to a far distant shore where God's Presence and Love are totally ignored. We become "center stage" and make godlike judgments by responding in the most deadly arrogance and authority. We cannot be in the heat and passion of anger and still be in God's Presence and Love. To all four degrees or conditions of anger, Jesus says there is a reckoning day of accountability.

Jesus is saying anger can be such a totalitarian emotion that it completely takes us over. As it assumes dominion and rule, we move away from Jesus and His love. James 1:20 says, "For the wrath of man does not achieve the righteousness of God." Paul states in Colossians 3:8, "Put aside anger, wrath, malice, slander and abusive speech from your mouth." He also says in

Ephesians 4:26–27 says, "Be angry, yet do not sin, do not let the sun go down on your anger and do not give the devil an opportunity." In other words, resolve all problems as quickly as possible. Jesus is exclaiming, "watch yourself and deal with your anger."

In the King James Version we have these words, "But I say unto you, everyone who is angry with his brother without cause" Matthew 5:22. There is a great difference between truly righteous anger against wicked and cruel acts, and angry, wrathful thoughts against those who do terrible deeds. For example, the tragedy of Bosnia, Rwanda, or India, does and should produce righteous outrage or anger but we must still watch our thoughts toward those who do such dastardly deeds. It is the old adage of "loving the sinner, yet hating the sin."

Then Jesus is saying too, "Be careful your anger is not way out of bounds for the deed done. Do not overact and allow Satan to enter in, distorting the facts and ignoring God's love." To project or transfer all my anger on someone who has not intentionally meant to offend is very common. Every time we react excessively in anger, there are other obscured reasons for our losing such control.

We know the amount of praying and loving that is needed if we are to respond as Jesus expects of us. He continues to love us unconditionally, and commands us, that by His grace and love, He wants to love through us. We are to persist in prayer until we do allow Him to love through us (Matt 5:43–48). One of God's greatest victories in us is the cleansing of anger and wrath we have toward someone so we can love them in God's love.

There is a very moving example I heard concerning a mother who told her story of finally being able love and forgive the man who raped and murdered her daughter. She spoke of how it took her time in prayer, and a lot of Jesus' love, to come to such a place of Calvary love for the man!

Jesus is teaching here that emotional murder is sinful and wrong, and any sinful attitude will be brought into accountability by the Holy Spirit. The Pharisees' inner hatred and anger was manifested in murdering Jesus. Though they did not do the actual deed, it was still "heart murder," which drove them to "physical murder."

One of the most powerful aspects of prayer is that if we will continue daily in prayer—real, genuine prayer—He will begin to show us how much like the worst sinner we actually are. Any restraint on us is God's precious grace through the Holy Spirit. Someone is praying for us somewhere, or we too would be out of the restraint of the Spirit of Love.

Learning to deal with our anger is one of the most vital issues in our life. Secular psychology is saying that we need to journal an hour a day, getting in touch with our feelings, to defuse our daily anger, of which we all have so much.

Actually, anger is a symptom of much that needs to be looked at in our life. When God allows it to surface, He wants us to look long and hard at the exposed emotion so that through Him we can confront our anger. One of the best ways of bringing anger to the light is journaling with the Holy Spirit, so He can throw His loving light on the situation. We need also, to "pray it out," using vocal prayer, so the Holy Spirit can direct our spoken words and give us his understanding. Many times, if we have been deeply sinned against, we will need to seek professional help in addition to much prayer and journaling. The main factor is that anger, any and all, must not be repressed, suppressed or denied. It must be recognized and dealt with. Forgiveness can then flow (Matt 6:9–15).

Jesus would have us learn to use anger for good and sin not with the emotion (Eph 4:26–27). Anger can push us out and away from God's love, unable to hear the voice of God, unable to obey and grow in grace. When anger is used for good, the emotion has been cleansed and the energy of love becomes a channel through which He can flow. A current example is the group of mothers called Mothers Against Drunk Drivers (MADD). Many of these mothers, who have lost a child because of a drunk driver, have used their anger in a redemptive way.

Then in this passage Jesus urges that where we need restitution, repentance, reconciliation we move in those healing directions (Matt 5:23–26). Matthew 5:23 says, "If your brother has ought against you"; Mark 11:25 reads "If you have anything against anyone, forgive, so your Father can forgive you." Jesus is saying that there must be the resolution of forgiveness in any and all offences.

In closing may I ask, are you up-to-date in all anger resolution today? Are there any grudges, any resentment, or any harsh opinions you need to confess as sin? Have you forgiven all sins of anger against you from others? Have you asked for forgiveness of your angry attitudes? As much as lies within, you, are you living in peace with all men and women (Rom 12:18)? Are you processing your anger in daily prayer?

During this week, ask the Holy Spirit to guide you and surface in you the anger with which He wants you to deal. Take time in prayer for the Holy Spirit to teach you and guide you. Respond in faith and trust, facing all He reveals, and Praise Him that "He that is in you is greater than He that is in the world" (1 John 4:4).

22

Ways to Handle Anger

He that is slow to anger is better than the mighty; and he
that ruleth his spirit than he that taketh a city.
Proverbs 16:32

THE LAST chapter centered on Jesus speaking of four of
the most dangerous human emotions (Matt 5:21–48).
We looked in particular at anger (Matt 5:21–26).

Jesus was interested in far more than the outward
conduct and outward deed. He was looking long and hard
at the inward conduct and inward deed. Knowing the
desperately wicked condition of our heart, He is saying be
careful, be very wise, and confront whatever you need to in
attitude because therein is "heart murder." This is produced
by anger. And anger unredeemed produces great harm and
havoc. "Heart murder" is done through allowing anger to
tongue-lash and demean another person, whether aloud or
silently. "Heart murder" is the result of great judgment and
a heart full of wrath against another. Psychologists' term for
this is survival rage.

Heart anger, for whatever reason, must be brought
under the control of the Holy Spirit with cleansing by
the power of the Holy Spirit (Jer 17:9–10; Jas 4:1–4).
Unresolved anger is highly destructive to our physical body,
as well as our spirit. For the sake of our health, we must
stay close to the Holy Spirit, so He can help us process our

anger, and bring it to the Cross of Jesus Christ for in-depth cleansing. Cleansed anger produces an energy that God can use (Eph 4:29).

Added to our own highly explosive sinful nature is the growing escalation of anger in our broken society. Daily there are dozens of examples in our community where anger has not been cleansed, and erupts in dangerous ways. Jesus is saying, "To walk with me, there must be a deep and constant cleansing by my Blood on your anger." The emotion of anger under the Holy Spirit's cleansing can be an agent for great good (Matt 21:12–13).

The serious question we all raise is "How do we allow the Holy Spirit to help us?" I want to list some ways Jesus can come to our aid in protecting us when we are angry.

- When you are angry, turn to Jesus at once, and ask for His help. The first few seconds in anger are the most crucial. Remember Jesus' words of admonishment that anger can get so out of hand, in a matter of minutes, that not only heart or attitudinal murder can take place, but physical murder can transpire. *Beware!*

- If you cannot get to the Holy Spirit at once, say nothing until you can get to God. Be aware of giving anger full reign. The perspective of the Holy Spirit will be different from your anger point of view that is removed from the Presence of Jesus.

- When we are angry, Jesus does not leave us. He is always available and accessible. But our anger pushes us away from Him, or it can, when we take matters into our own hands.

- Start to pray in the midst of the anger, as soon as possible. Satan will be right there to whip up the fires of anger, and attempt to get them out of control as soon as he can. Do not allow the emotions to take over, but cry out to the Holy Spirit to empower your will to do rightly no matter how your emotions rage.

- If necessary, say to the person with whom you are angry "I am angry, and I cannot speak anymore now. I need time to think and pray about this, we will talk later."

- Name your anger, own it, admit it, and confess it to Jesus. Let denial be removed through the Holy Spirit so that deep honesty can take place.

- Write out your feelings in your journal. This allows the Holy Spirit to process the entire experience with you. He will dialogue with you.

- Listen to His voice and word, both through the Scriptures and the inner voice of the Holy Spirit.

- If restitution is necessary, do it. Obey.

- Keep short accounts with Jesus and with others. Process until resolved. Do not let feelings simmer and escalate as eruption is inevitable. Deal with the issue as soon as possible.

- Study Galatians 5:22–26 for the qualities of the Holy Spirit in you.

Only in the sacred confines of the Prayer Closet can the precious Holy Spirit get a hold of our unruly and self-centered emotions. He wants to alter our anger manifested in heart and tongue murder, as we pour out our pain and anguish to Him. He will begin to teach us how to let go of these bitter emotions. To give them to Jesus in and through the Holy Spirit is one of the Spirit's major aids to help His people. To receive His blessed Presence and soak in His mercy and grace brings release if we will go His way, and allow Him time to minister to us.

23

From Self-Control to God-Control

For if you love them which love you, what
reward have ye? Do not even the publicans
do the same? Be ye therefore perfect, even as
your Father which is in heaven is perfect.
Matthew 5:46–48

WE HAVE been in an absolutely thrilling experiment, a Prayer Experiment, in which we are seeking to allow the Holy Spirit to bring us into a deep alignment with His Word. *The Sermon on the Mount* has been our foundational Scripture. We have seen many wonderful answers come out of this experiment.

My mother used to say, "We take prayer as Jesus taught it, into the laboratory of our daily lives, and under the microscope of obedience, we carry out His formulas for answered prayer. If we will be obedient to the formula, He will bring answers as sure as His word."

We have been taking Jesus literally at His word in the *Sermon on the Mount,* and the results are amazing.

Jesus is speaking constantly of the deep need for our inner attitudes, or thought life, to be in oneness with our outer action. Where there is no conflict between the inner and outer life, prayers will be answered. There will be no hypocrisy, no dishonesty of any kind, no show or pretense, and the results will be revolutionary.

The real seat of power or powerlessness is the attitude of our inner thought life. James 1:6–8 says, "Man that is double-minded is unstable in all his ways, let not that man expect anything from the Lord." Jesus is saying that real faith and trust evolves when the inner life and outer life are in harmony and oneness. Actually, the only prayers that are answered are those that come from an inner life that is deeply obedient to God's laws. The outer life will be easily and naturally in harmony with the inner. Whenever there is conflict between the two, there is a hindrance of God's will (Luke 6:44–49).

We want now to continue our study of Matthew 5 by looking at verses 27–32. Jesus is speaking of the second deadly, dangerous emotion and its great potential for evil. That emotion is *lust*. He says, "Do not commit adultery," but what Jesus is emphasizing is at the point of emotional or heart adultery. He is saying that lust is so highly charged that whatever stirs up lust must be eliminated. Jesus is saying, "Get out of any emotional or physical adultery now!" In other words remove yourself from whatever it may be—the eye, the hand, cut it off.

To lust after a man or woman, is to have committed adultery with that person in your heart (Matt 5:28). The inward act is every bit as sinful as the outward act. We are to literally nip in the bud any and all emotional adultery. Keep out of sin's way. The Holy Spirit will guide you and direct you into safety. If your lust is uncontrollable there is professional help for sexual addiction.

The tragedy today is that even Christian people are being destroyed because they will not be obedient to God. The force of the sexual revolution has destroyed the moral fabric of our nation, and each of us must be on our guard through much prayer and obedience to the Holy Spirit

(Prov 2:10–19). None of us is beyond the enemy's plan to attack in the area of sexual lust.

You may say to me, "Margaret, I am not into any physical or emotional adultery, so what does this passage say to me?"

Thank the dear Lord that you are not into physical or emotional adultery. He is in deep control of you at the point of this dangerous emotion. That is wonderful.

But I would like to reflect on an aspect of lust that is so detrimental to the Christian. What I refer to here is the need for control in prayer, a possession of power through the prayer life. Our possessiveness to have our own way is deeply embedded in each one of us. This possessiveness is lust in action.

We know that there is an appropriate and an inappropriate way to get our sexual needs met. It is also very inappropriate to try to use power-control in our prayer life to get our prayers answered. Sad to say, it is done often in the prayer life. I believe it is Andrew Murray who said, "There is much that must be taken from us, before God can really begin to flow through us."

The cleansing of the lust of control in prayer is much needed in every one of us. It is common to take our need for power and control into our prayer life and use the enormous energy of lust or control to try to get what we want, when we want it. Many people stay on that "control trek" and never ever really get off of it, and into the deep things of God. Self-knowledge is one of God's supreme gifts (John 16:7–16).

Of course, lust will disguise itself in any way it can, and come out as a disguised need to control God and others. This is the reason many people in the secular world are leery of what we mean by "prayer power." They have seen people with obvious power-control issues in their life so that they have no confidence in the prayers of these Christian people.

Anger left to fester and become more agitated hurts our prayer life. In the same way, lust or inflated control and arrogance toward God must be acknowledged and dealt with at some time.

Someone has said that we all have authority issues. How true this is. The most transforming prayer that we can pray is for the Holy Spirit to surface whatever He wants to bring to our attention. Oh, that we might humbly ask Jesus to cleanse us from all control and power issues, as we process with Him all our sin and need (Ps 19:12–14).

Even if our self-will is given to God, the best we know, we must be very transparent with Jesus and very careful that we are not presumptuous and assertive to get our own way. We must be very careful how we petition God to do something. Our self-love is so strong. It takes a lot of prayer to *not* tell Him in detail all we want, in much persuasion and emotion, and then not to be angry and disappointed when it does not come as we planned.

It also takes a lot of prayer for Him to be able to trust us enough to send the details He wants to use, and it will be alright with us. Actually, there are very few people in that thoughtful a prayer life. Allowing God to give what He sees fit to send, and knowing it will be joyfully received is profound indeed! What a thrilling experience to allow the Holy Spirit to reveal God's will and be content with it (1 Cor 2:6–16)!

Mother used to say, "God has a hundred thousand ways to meet our needs." We need to relax, hang loose, and allow Him opportunity to be His gloriously creative best.

He will often do differently than we expect. Leave the *how and when* to Him. Beware of becoming demanding in your zeal and passion. Do not be presumptuous and feed your need for control and power. Rather, let the Holy

Spirit give His and God's point of view. Let the Holy Spirit and God meet within you and reveal His truth. The plain fact is we do not love His will that much because it takes great pruning and great cleansing to bring us gladly to His will. One of our main tragedies is we do not give Him time enough to reveal Himself. Nor do we give Him time enough to cleanse us daily. We need to allow the Holy Spirit much more time to share God's compassion with us.

The great Christians have spoken of "Holy Unconcern" or the "Abandonment to Him of how, when, and where." It requires spending more time listening to Him and loving Him than anything else, certainly more than telling Him what to do and how and when to do it.

How we need to soak in His loving Presence, gazing at Him rather than begging and pleading for Him to do certain things we want. The need for God to do it our way is far stronger than any of us know. We need to be much more in Jesus' Presence, that He might show us *our tragic flaw of control*, even in prayer (Jas 4:1–3; 2 Cor 3:17–18). Let me share an example of the control issue in prayer.

Years ago God birthed an intense burden for someone in me. The Holy Spirit presented me with insight into what He wanted to do in restoring and making this person whole. Much prayer ensued. Human prayer, mingled with the prayers of the Holy Spirit, flowed in great intensity over an extended period of time.

Since my time investment was intense and often, I did not realize how much of "me" was telling God how to work it out in a certain way. Great little planner that I am, I thought I would help God along by telling Him how to do it all. The depth of my control was lost to me, because it is so much a part of me and my self-will. Because there was great intensity in the praying, I figured it was out beyond my self-will and was God.

Mercifully, out of God's great love for me and the person for whom I was praying, God was able to do some things, but only as He has revealed my control or lust in prayer. I repented as God began to really work. The Holy Spirit told me to be careful in the future not to fall prey to pushing my will over His will.

Praying for others requires a careful listening always to the Holy Spirit and allowing Him to correct us in all areas, especially our need for power or control in prayer.

I want to close with a bottom line of wisdom from St. Theresa of Avila, "True humility consists in our being satisfied with what is given us, in being ready for what the Lord desires to do with us, and happy that He should do it." May you and I not only avoid all possible emotional adultery this week, but also experience a profound death to our self-centeredness. Let us allow God to be God, and in our praying, keep surrendering all, everything and everyone to Him and His good pleasure.

24

"Divine Realization"—God's Gift to Us in Prayer

For He is our peace, who hath made
both one, and hath broken down
the middle wall of partition between us.
Ephesians 2:14

P SALM 115:3 says, "Our God is in the Heavens, He does whatever He pleases." This powerful verse needs to become part of the fiber of our soul and spirit that we might continually lay down all God-defying attitudes of control that go all the way back to the Garden of Eden. Adam and Eve wanted things their way, but they did not succeed with their need for power.

My father was a Methodist pastor in southeastern Kentucky when I was a small child. On some Saturday afternoons he would invite my sister, Edith, and my brother, Wayne, to go with him to the next town to run errands.

Daddy might do some shopping, but the real treat was that at the end of necessary errands, he would buy us a 10-cent bag of candy. Our problem was that Edith always wanted to carry the bag and dole out to Wayne and me a few meager pieces, while she carried the sack.

I can still see her, with her fat, bouncy curls clutching the sack, as Wayne and I were begging for candy. Daddy saw that this would never do, so he arranged a system; Edith one Saturday, Margaret the next and then Wayne, since he was the oldest, would carry the sack the third Saturday—of course, you understand that neither Wayne nor I ever wanted to carry the sack!

Only much time spent with Jesus cleanses us from the sin of control. He helps us to see how self-focused we are, and how desperately we need Him, and how much we want our own way.

Emmet Fox, whose writings on the Sermon on the Mount have helped thousands of people, has this to say about control:

> When we undertake to bring about particular events or conditions or particular solutions to our problems, I call it "outlining." It is wanting God to fill it in according to our desires and outline. Don't seek to select exact arrangements that will come about, or the course that things will take. If you make up your mind very firmly that you are going to get a particular thing in a particular way, you may get it, but may bitterly regret it later on. (Ps 106:13–15)[1]

We believe consecrated prayer on our part does no outlining but only joyously surrenders to any set of conditions He wants to create. He and He alone knows His divine plan. We learn to not murmur or complain about His will. The author of the following quote is not known to me but says this so very well. "We find it very hard to believe that God knows all, and what He plans for us is best. We prefer to follow our fallen reason or our own defective sight. What we can see and what we can understand is very, very limited. God knows all and sees all."

Now we want to look at Matthew 5:33–37. Jesus is saying here for us to keep our hearts and minds sensitive

---

1. Fox, *The Sermon on the Mount*, 172–82.

and responsive to the inspiration of the Holy Spirit. Watch your conversation, and the words you say, that you do not speak too authoritatively and smugly.

Many serious Christians have found the time of simply being still and waiting on God to be life changing. As we learn to listen to Him He speaks to our heart and mind showing us whatever we need to perceive within ourselves—whether of doubt and unbelief, self-love or self-will.

Emmet Fox has some strong words of counsel for us concerning this passage when we pray.

> Don't make your mind up in advance, as to what you shall do or not do, where you shall be or not be today or tomorrow. When you crystallize this determination by a solemn act of the will, like a vow, you are not leaving yourself open to the action of the Paraclete. You are, by that act shutting Him out (Jas 4:13–17).
>
> If we are to receive Jesus, His Personhood, with all His attributes, we must not say in advance what we will and will not do, but stay open to the indwelling Jesus constantly, moment by moment.
>
> We grieve Him by preventing His action; we are shut off from the ever fresh energy and action of God that is Life in Jesus. He yearns over us moment by moment, to fellowship and commune with us.
>
> The result of this is spiritual stagnation, a failure to allow Him to flow through us now. The main reason for this consists of spiritual pride and self-righteousness.[2]

These statements by Emmet Fox are extremely helpful, and we are grateful to him for showing us how much we live

---

2. Fox, *The Sermon on the Mount*, 74.

out of self-assertion and self-will, rather than the inspiration of the Holy Spirit.

The third harmful emotion is *pride* or *arrogance*. The place of daily prayer is an opening to the blessed Holy Spirit to surface our haughtiness so that we can repent and cry out to God to cleanse us of this terrible sin.

Of course, this passage, Matthew 5:33–37, says also that we are to enter into ordinary business engagements, but as all the interpreters of the Sermon on the Mount say, Jesus is here speaking of spiritual realities; but Jesus says in another passage "We are to render to Caesar what is Caesar's" (Matt 22:21). But in Matthew 5:33–37 Jesus is speaking of spiritual attitudes of the inner life, the source of our being. One of the reformations of the daily prayer closet is the Holy Spirit seeking to bring us to more and more dependency on the Holy Spirit and less self-sufficiency.

The asking of the Holy Spirit to come forth in prayer (Rom 8:26) is often in deep groanings that cannot be uttered. They go too deep to speak. He wants to train us to give Him Lordship, in our thought life and prayer life, moment by moment, so it is up to Him to pray the way only He can pray. Some years ago the Holy Spirit guided us in prayer group into asking the Holy Spirit to pray through us, with no flesh or natural man trying to take over the prayer. Many of us were already entering into that, in private prayer. More and more silence has developed in the prayer group as a result in which there is the silent groanings of the Holy Spirit being expressed within the heart.

This has made a tremendous difference to all of us privately and corporately. So much prayer is of our own making, not His, but we are being trained to "give over" to Him in prayer, more and more, that we might "give over" to Him moment by moment. The main requirement is a *listening* to Him that comes out of *denying* ourself that He might pray in our hearts, while we learn to stay in close touch with the Holy Spirit.

There is a perfect Biblical example of Matthew 5:33–37 that is found in John 20:1–18. Here we find an example that best describes the moment by moment inspiration of the Holy Spirit, which is called *Divine Realization*, by the great people of prayer of past years.

Mary's realizations were tainted by her human limitation of understanding and capacity. But as she lingered in the place where He had been—as we linger in our place of prayer—He shows Himself to her. In her realizations of the moment, she felt Jesus was lost to her and permanently missing, but when Jesus revealed Himself, she saw how mistaken she had been. He was alive when she thought Him dead. He was present to her when she thought Him missing.

As Jesus spoke her name, she perceived correctly—Jesus is alive and here, and she moved into His Reality and Perception rather than being stuck in her own. She knew Him so well and loved Him totally. She was open and responsive as well as she knew. He cleared her vision and understanding and the true state of affairs was revealed to her. Her human realization became Jesus' Divine Realization or Perspective. It is all in being in His Presence until our realizations are altered by Him (Matt 11:28–30).

Momma used to say, "We are either a Divine Demonstration or a human display." Divine Demonstration comes out of Divine Realization! Human display comes out of human realization!

May you and I keep open to Him, not making our own plans out of human understanding, but so tuned in to Him we move moment by moment under His guidance. John Baillie, the great Scottish preacher, once said, "If I thought that God was going to grant me all my prayers simply for the asking, without ever passing them under His own gracious review, without ever bringing to bear upon them His own greater wisdom, I think there would be very few prayers that I should dare to pray."

May you and I walk in flexibility and openness to His voice and leading in these thrilling days. Let us not predetermine what we will do or say, but open ourselves to His continual inspiration through the Holy Spirit.

Pride and arrogance are so apt to dominate our self-life that it will capture our ability to hear the still small voice of the Holy Spirit. Daily repentance and a growing denial of self needs to be more apparent in all our lives.

25

Overcome Evil with Good

*Be not overcome of evil,
but overcome evil with good.*
Romans 12:21

MATTHEW CHAPTERS 5 through 7 have been the basis for this tremendous *Prayer Experiment*. Hopefully this has been a life changing experience for you, as it has been for our praying community, by bringing you into more joy and peace, with more prayer authority. We have sought through the Holy Spirit, to be more obedient and true in our inner soul and spirit. Our thought life has been remolded by Jesus' words in chapters 5, 6, and 7 in the Gospel of Matthew. Our self-life has been soaked in God's love more and we have a growing passion to be like Him!

He has honored this study with greater hunger for Him, and for more answers to prayer, particularly for greater answers in very difficult situations. He has been given greater access and been wonderfully triumphant.

We will look at the last Scripture, Matthew 5:38–48, to gather the biblical prayer laws from this passage. Our fourth emotion, *retaliation* is not giving back to a person what they have given us.

Jesus is saying that the old law was whatever man did to man; he should be ready to suffer the same thing. If he killed a person, he would be killed, if he put another's eye out, his eye would be taken. In other words, to get even, to pay back, to even things up somehow or other, when we have been hurt or suffered injustice, we give back what we have been given. This is the essence of retaliation. Jesus says, "Though this is the old law, I have a new law to give you." The old "getting even" must stop. Revenge is a canceling out of God's love being released in the situation. There is no healing for either side without God's love.

Jesus reverses the attitude of getting even and states, when someone injures you, instead of paying him back in the same way he hurt you, do the opposite thing, forgive and set him free, and set yourself free too. Break the cycle of evil begetting more evil, and by what psychology calls a "paradoxical injunction," do exactly the opposite which is to love, to forgive, to set free and thereby overcome evil with good (Rom 12:17–21; 1 Pet 3:8–9).

What does it mean to not "resist evil"? Let us respond to that question by making some basic statements about retaliation. Emmet Fox says, "To resist not evil means we rob the incident of its power by turning quickly and deeply to Jesus. Get into His love immediately, when the offense comes, so He can dissipate the anger and retaliation by His love."[1] That could not be better said. Get to Jesus and His love to break the cycle of evil for evil. To overcome evil with good we must live in Jesus' Presence.

We believe so deeply in this, that it may well be the culmination of our prayer processing, rather than the initial steps. Let me make some statements that serve as the basis for overcoming evil with good.

1. We do give situations power and control over us by obsessing over the problem in our minds and emotions. Personal hurt is one of the major obstacles that prevent us from coming to Jesus. We

---

1. Fox, *The Sermon on the Mount*, 70–71.

wrestle with it. We agonize over it instead of inviting Father, Son, and Holy Spirit to enter into this battle with us. We love to stay focused on our personal pain. "After all, this happened to me!" Of course, the enemy of our soul and spirit is right in the midst of it to tell you that God does not care about you and has not been faithful to you.

2. If we have been waiting with our beloved Lord in the inner room of prayer daily, we are much more conditioned to bring everything including our terrible pain to Him. There at his feet we can pour it out audibly, honestly, wholeheartedly, and speak exactly how we feel. Hold nothing back; lay it all out to Him.

3. In all circumstances whether happy or sad, there are four elements that must be considered. We have mentioned these points before but let us look at these areas in more detail.

   a. First, ask Him to show you your part in what has happened. It is so easy to blame or shame someone else, and not take personal ownership what we have done. Ask the Holy Spirit to reveal your personal contribution in what has happened. We do understand that in sexual abuse with children they have done nothing to warrant such conduct.

   b. Then ask the Holy Spirit to show you the other person's part. Allow Him time enough to reveal where this person is locked into his or her pain.

   c. Then ask the Holy Spirit what Satan is seeking to do to you. We know his pattern is to kill, steal, and destroy (John 10:10).

d. Finally, what is God's part in this circumstance? What is He seeking to teach you about yourself and Him? What lessons in love and forgiveness is He endeavoring to bring about in you? This prayer processing is life changing. Time must be allowed to be with God to learn to hear Him closely and truly, but how wondrous the illumination of the Holy Spirit's way of thinking is to us—what comfort, clarity, and wisdom.

Listen to the Holy Spirit and what He gives you to do, to say, or to be in response to what He is saying. Be sure to try the spirits to see if they are from God (1 John 4:1). If you know an older, wiser person who is faithful in prayer, contact him or her and listen to what they say. This is a life time journey to learn to discern if what we are hearing is the Holy Spirit or what you or I may be saying. Time and space does not permit me to share the hundreds of situations our praying community has experienced alone or corporately in waiting on God and receiving His eternal Word and guidance.

Getting out beyond personal pain through being with the Holy Spirit will take time. I know of no better way to get to know the Godhead in a more personal way than this. The byproduct of a deepening self-knowledge is beyond expression. The saints say without self-knowledge we can have no God knowledge.

If we truly want Jesus' love to be released in a situation, He will be released in a mighty way if we will be obedient to His directions. At this moment we begin to pray for Jesus' love to flow through us to the person who has caused us such pain. This becomes *the prayer of the heart*. The prayer of the heart is what we truly trust God to do. Unhurried time in God's Presence is necessary to discover what we truly want, and we find that it is what He wants for us. As He begins to move through our heart in love our attitude of retaliation dissipates.

There is nothing anymore exciting than to see Jesus move in love toward all those who have persecuted us. How He enjoys responding in love. May you and I take the *Jesus Way, the Calvary Road*, with a *baptism* of Calvary Love to pour through us.[2] Then we will stand back and see the blessing of prayers answered in our lives and in our land.

It has been awesome to look at these glorious verses, and know He stands ready to fulfill the promises if we will walk in Holy Spirit obedience.

This Prayer Experiment can never be over. It simply progresses to evermore profound levels of spiritual understanding and power in the Holy Spirit. May you and I not feel we have "done it" or "we've arrived," but rather yearn for the dimensions of God's love we have never experienced before (Eph 3:14–21).

May we realize that it is in the Prayer Closet alone with Father, Son and Holy Spirit that the God-life begins to be allowed to quicken our inner life. He so wants to live through us as we move out into our daily challenges. May we walk in loving obedience to the Lord Jesus Christ as He empowers us to allow Him to live the Sermon on the Mount through us.

---

2. Hessin, *The Calvary Road*, 29–36.

Bibliography

Conley, William J. SJ. "Experiences of Darkness in Directed Retreats," in *Notes on the Spiritual Exercises of St. Ignatius of Loyola*, edited by David L. Fleming, S.J., 108–14. St. Louis, MO: Review for Religious, 1983.

Fox, Emmet. *The Sermon on the Mount*. New York: Harper and Row, Publishers, 1934.

Grou, Nicholas. *How To Pray*. London: Burns Oats & Washbourne LTD. 1928.

Hession, Roy. *The Calvary Road*. Philadelphia: Christian Literature Crusade, 1950.

Hurnard, Hannah. *God's Transmitters*. Wheaton Illinois: Tyndale House, 1983.

———. *The Winged Life*. Balkerne Gardens, Colchester, 1958.

Kelsey, Morton. *The Other Side of Silence: Part Four—The Use of Images in Meditation*. New York: Paulist Press, 1976.

Law, William and Dave Hunt, ed. *The Power of the Spirit*. Ft. Washington, Pennsylvania: Christian Literature Crusade, 1971.

Therkelsen, Margaret. *The Love Exchange*. Eugene, Oregon: Wipf and Stock Publishers, 2003.

Welch, Mary. *What Wilt Thou?: Three Steps to Creative Praying*. Henderson, Texas: Park Printing Company, 1952.